Marie L. Logan

Oil paintings
2007–2010

Alexandra von Stueckchen

Published by CordaNobelo Publishing.
Distributed through Createspace.com

Library of Congress Cataloging-in-Publication Data: for ordering information see back cover. Publisher can be reached at Publisher@CordaNobelo.com

Also by Alexandra von Stueckchen:
"Rupert Hart: Watercolor Nudes"

Artist's Statement

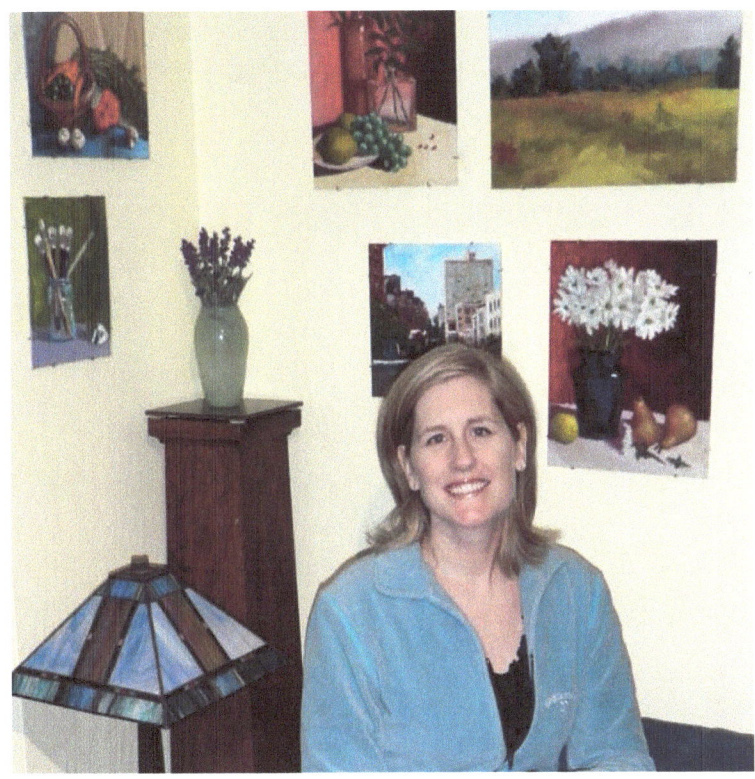

I began making art in earnest as a child, when at age five I created huge murals on my bedroom walls with markers and crayons, much to my parents' surprise and dismay. Luckily, they remained supportive of my budding talent. I took a Saturday art class at the Kendall School of Design in Grand Rapids and studied Commercial Art in high school, but then dropped my formal study of art in favor of more practical endeavors in college. I was inspired by an Impressionism exhibit I saw at the Art Institute of Chicago as a young girl, and art has always remained an avocation for me.

I have been interested in many forms of art over the years including sculpture in stone and clay and jewelry making. This foray into oil painting was sparked by the rediscovery of some oil paints and materials I had inherited many years ago from my artist grandmother, Helen Logan. She made paintings inspired by the western landscape and ran the Logan Gallery in Tucson, Arizona. Painting combines my love of nature and art, so it is truly a joy for me.

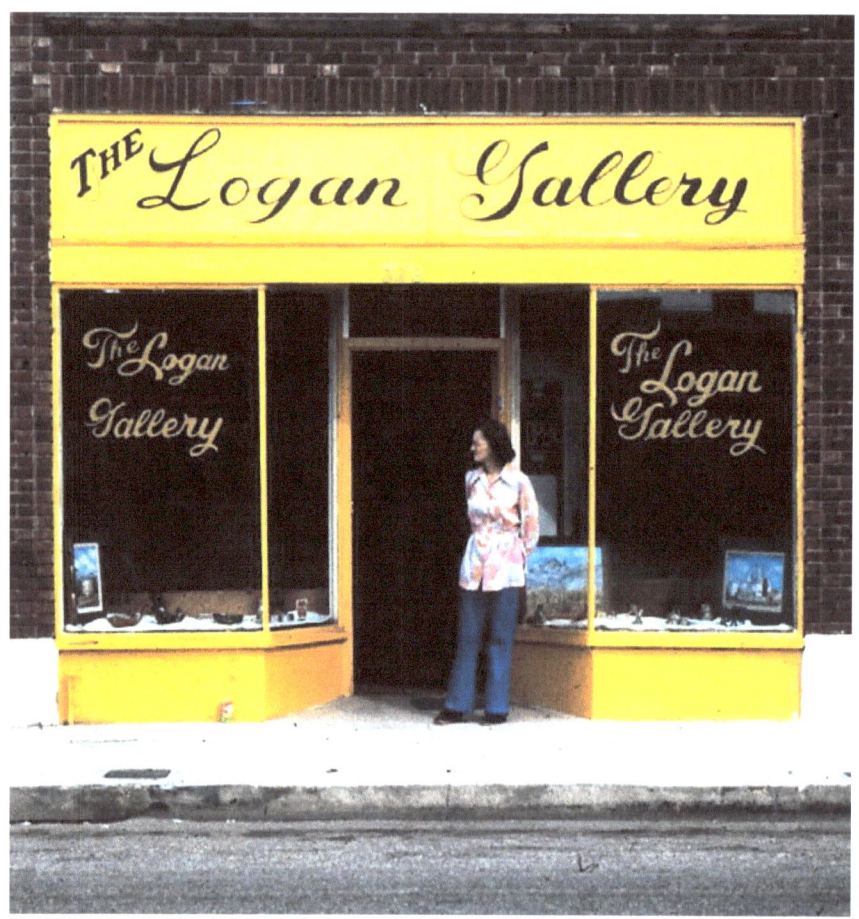

My grandmother Helen outside the Logan Gallery

Three paintings in this collection were made in 2007. Ocean Beach Kite was my first painting painted entirely with my grandmother Helen's 30-year old paints and pure intuition, as I had no training whatsoever in oil painting. This was painted for my father and mother for

Christmas that year in honor of my grandmother. The next painting was done for my brother to commemorate a visit he made to see me in California and it's called Lands End; he now owns that painting, as well. The next painting was made for myself and it is called Cement Ship at Sunset. It is my largest scale painting to date and it resides over the fireplace in my home. This is a sunset that my parents and I actually saw during a visit they made in December 2006, and it really was as brilliant as I painted it.

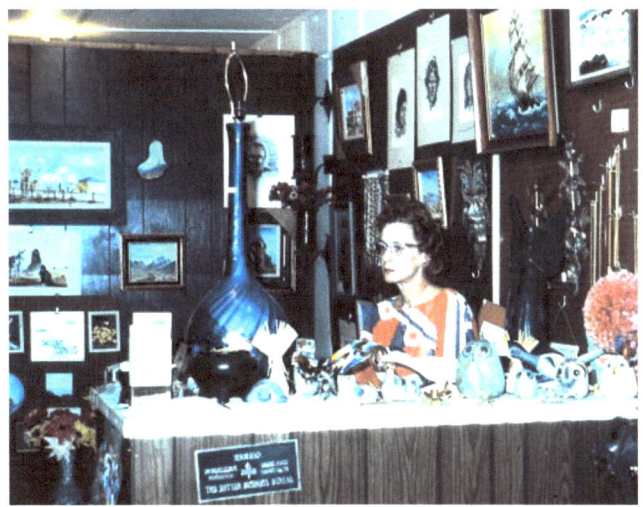

Helen in her gallery

I didn't paint again due to lack of studio space until I was inspired during the Santa Cruz Open Studios Art Tour in 2009, when I realized I could paint outdoors. I am fortunate to have found a wonderful local mentor in the Impressionist style - Barbara Bailey-Porter. On weekends you will find me painting either in the studio or outdoors "plein air." I painted the remaining 43 paintings between November 2009 and November 2010 and I hope to keep painting for a long time to come.

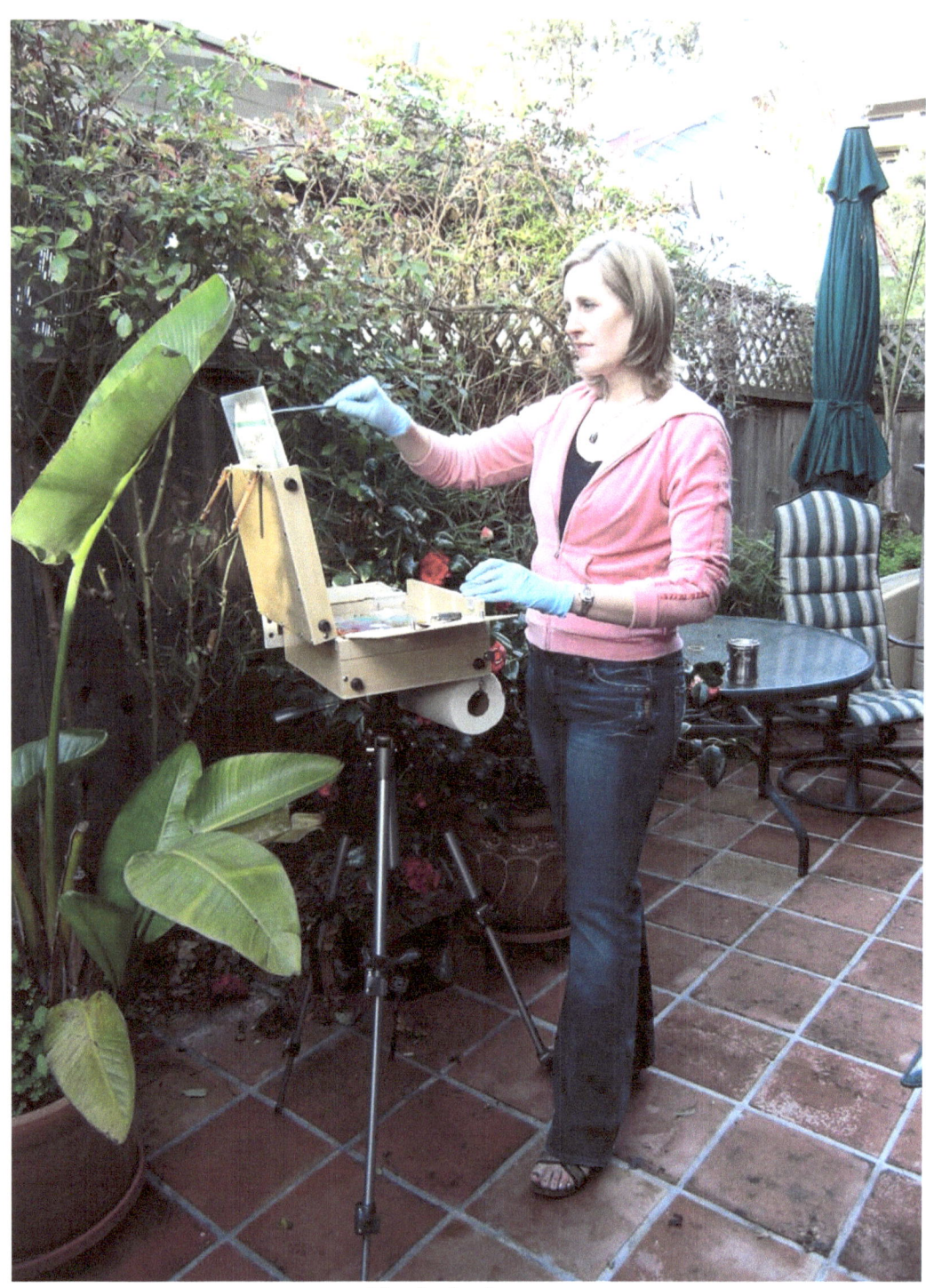

Marie L. Logan

The Plates

(in chronological order)

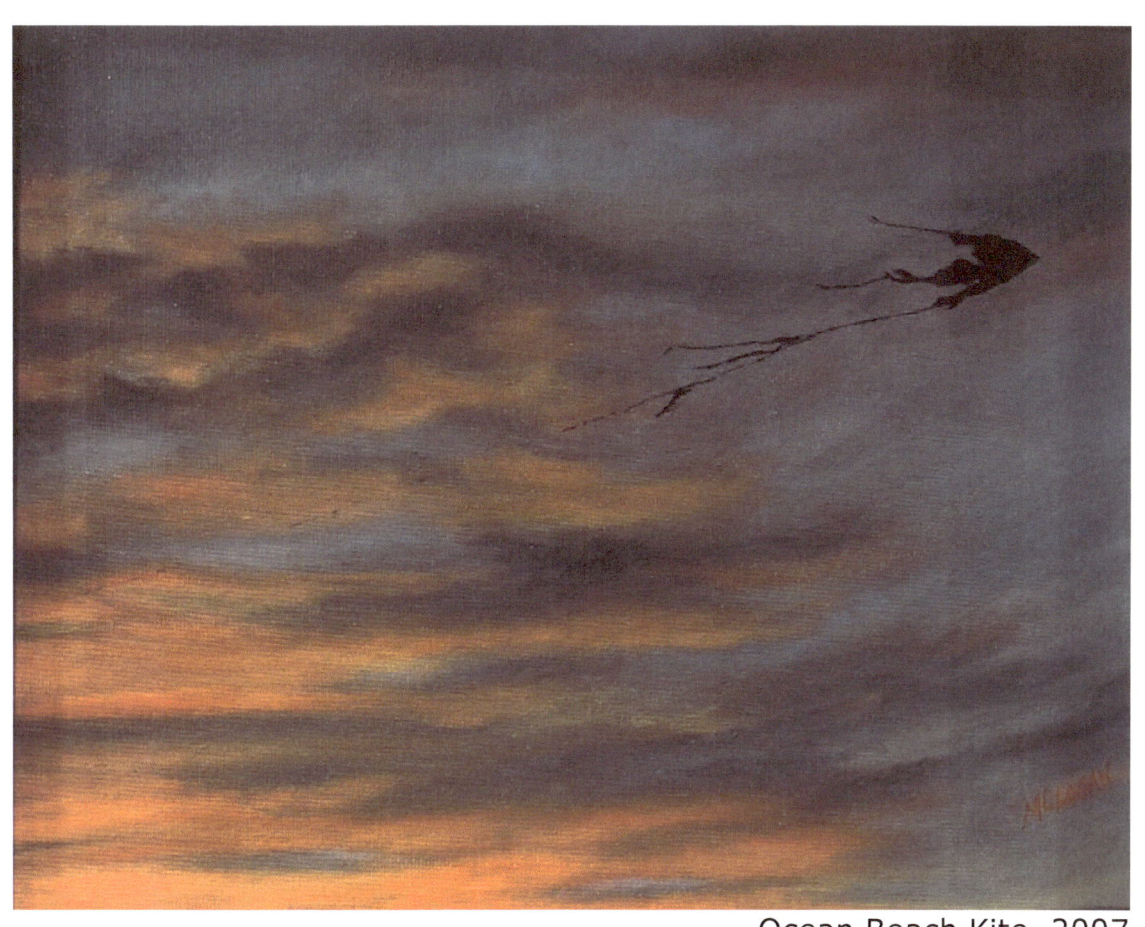

Ocean Beach Kite, 2007

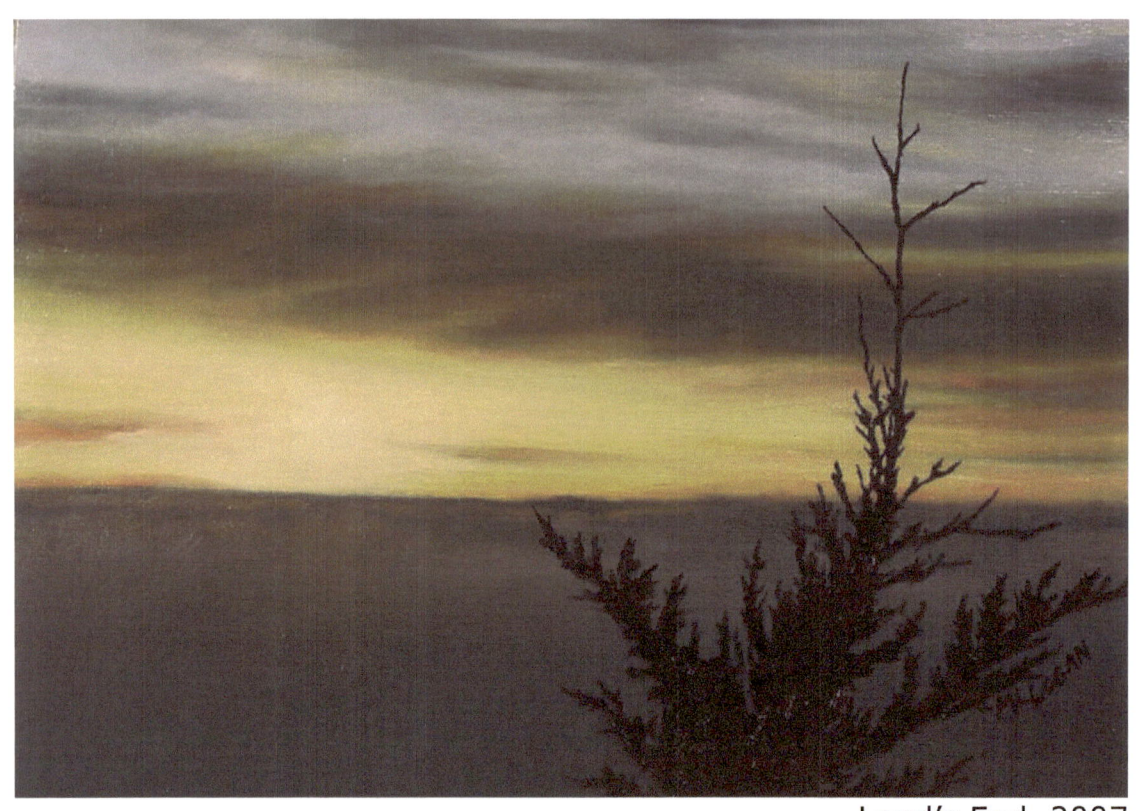

Land's End, 2007

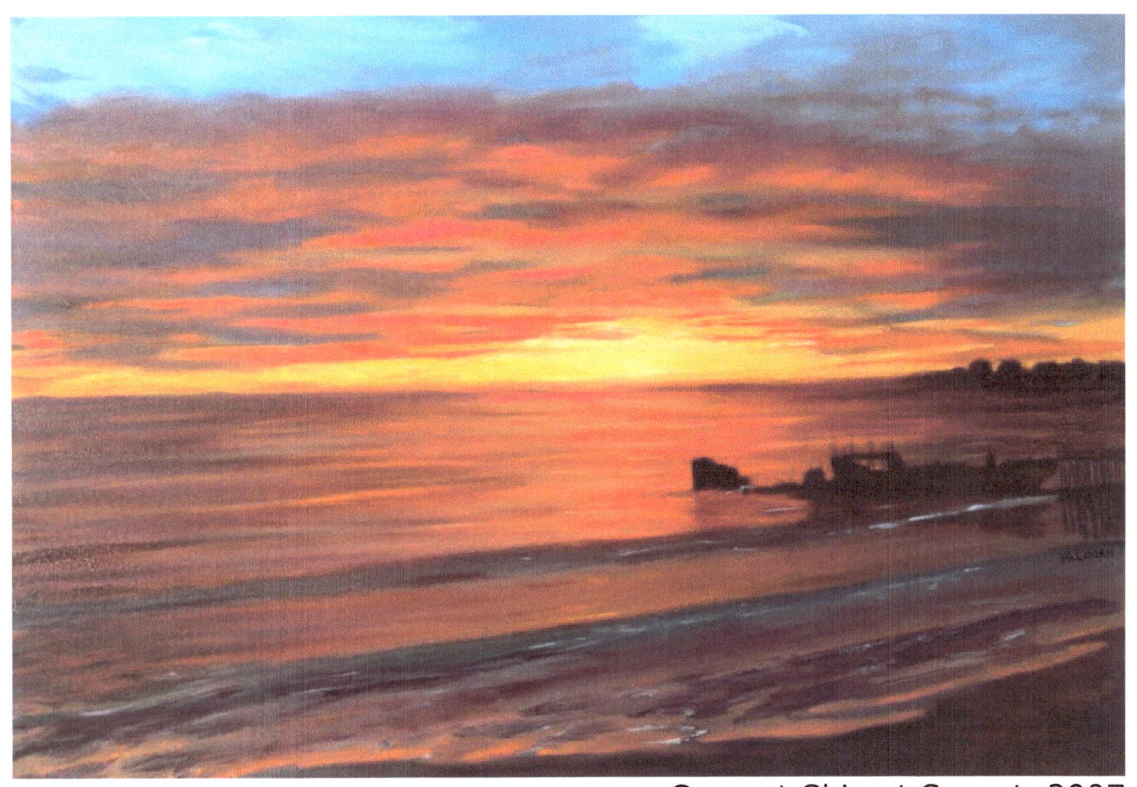

Cement Ship at Sunset, 2007

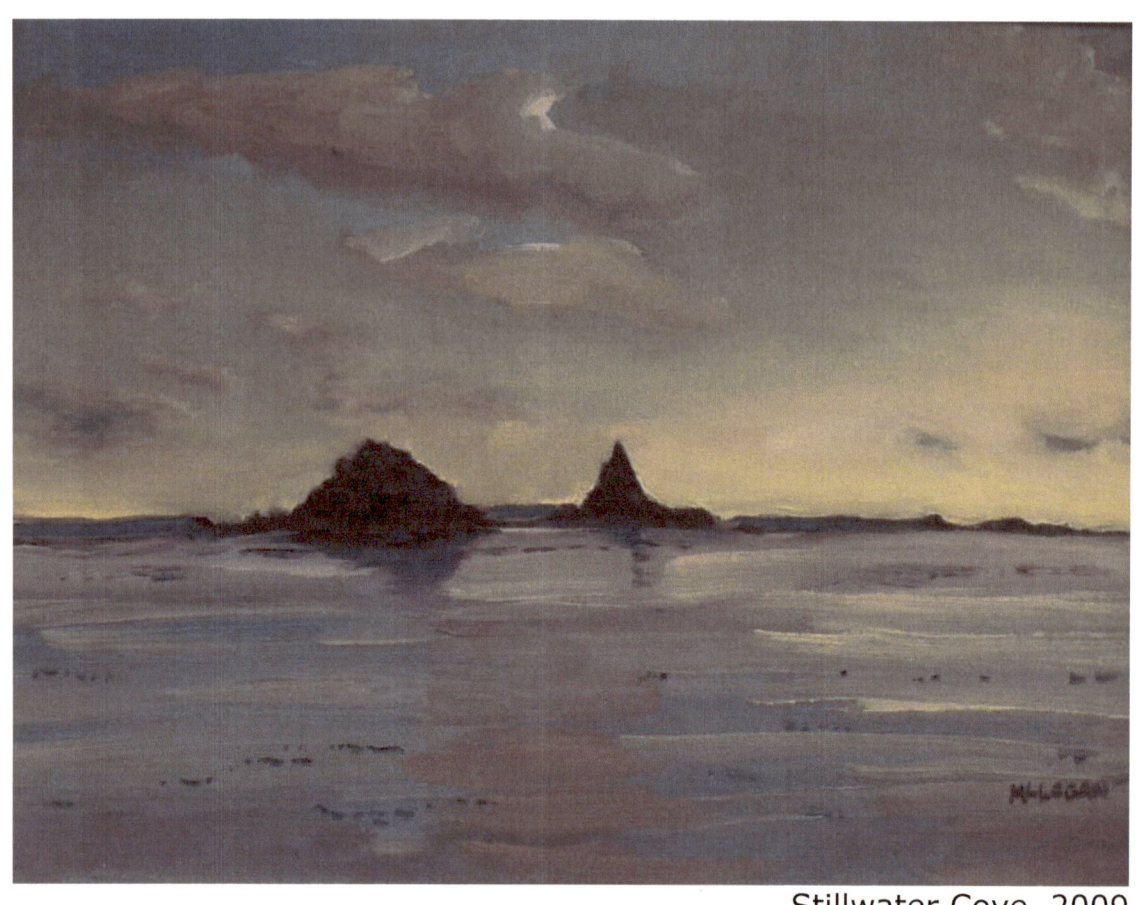

Stillwater Cove, 2009

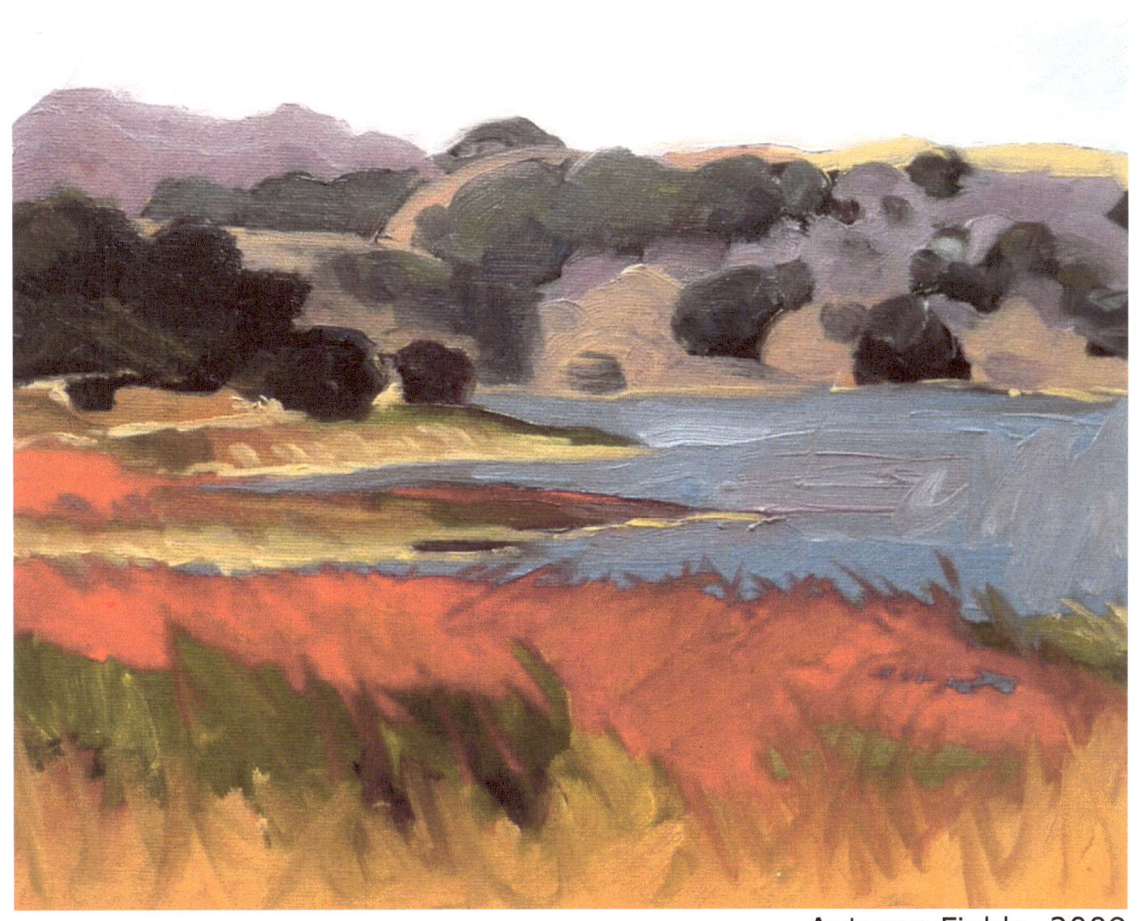

Autumn Fields, 2009

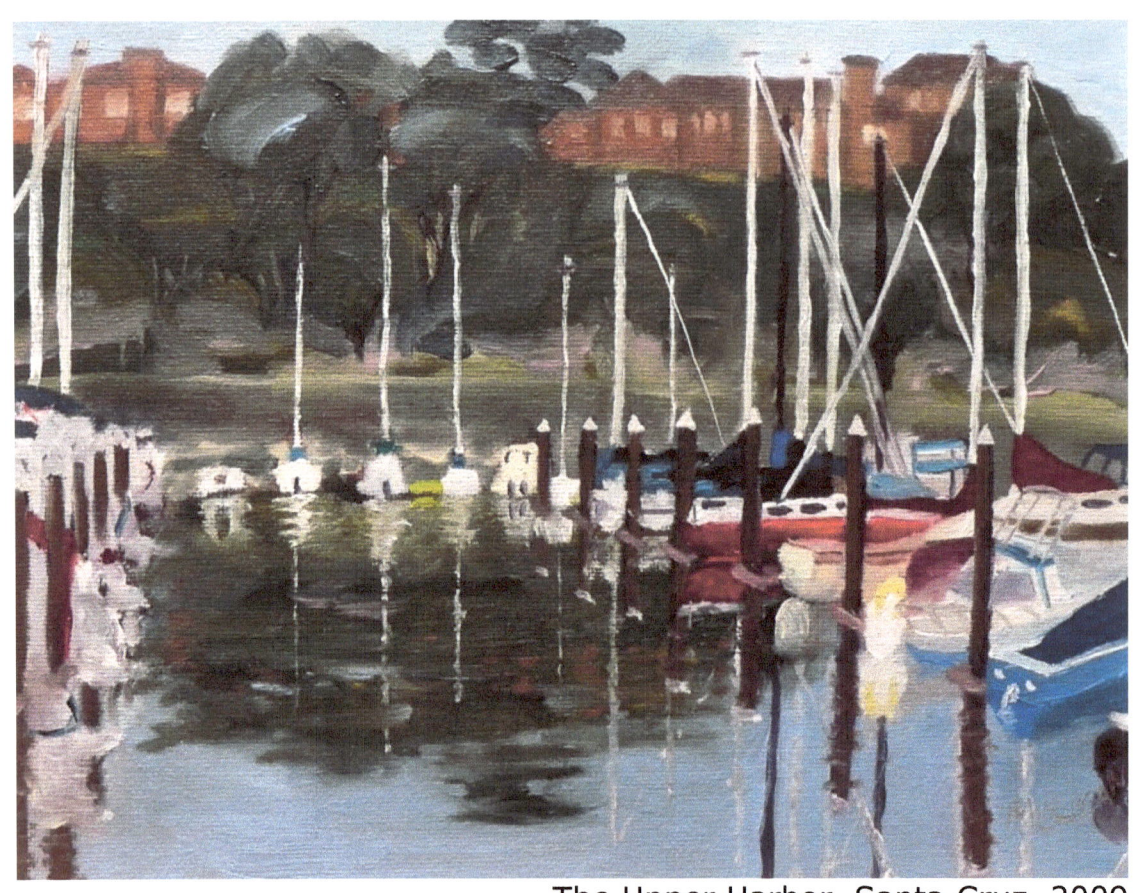

The Upper Harbor, Santa Cruz, 2009

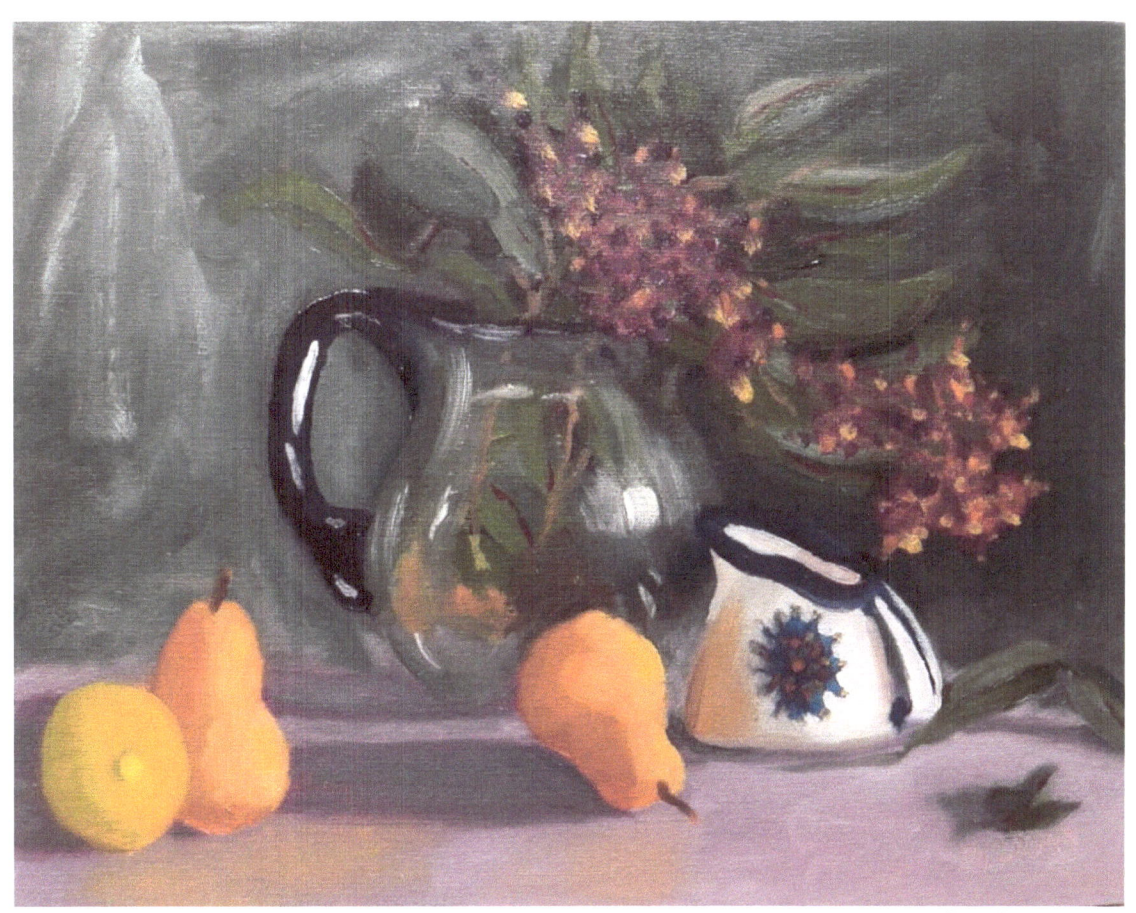

First Still Life, 2009

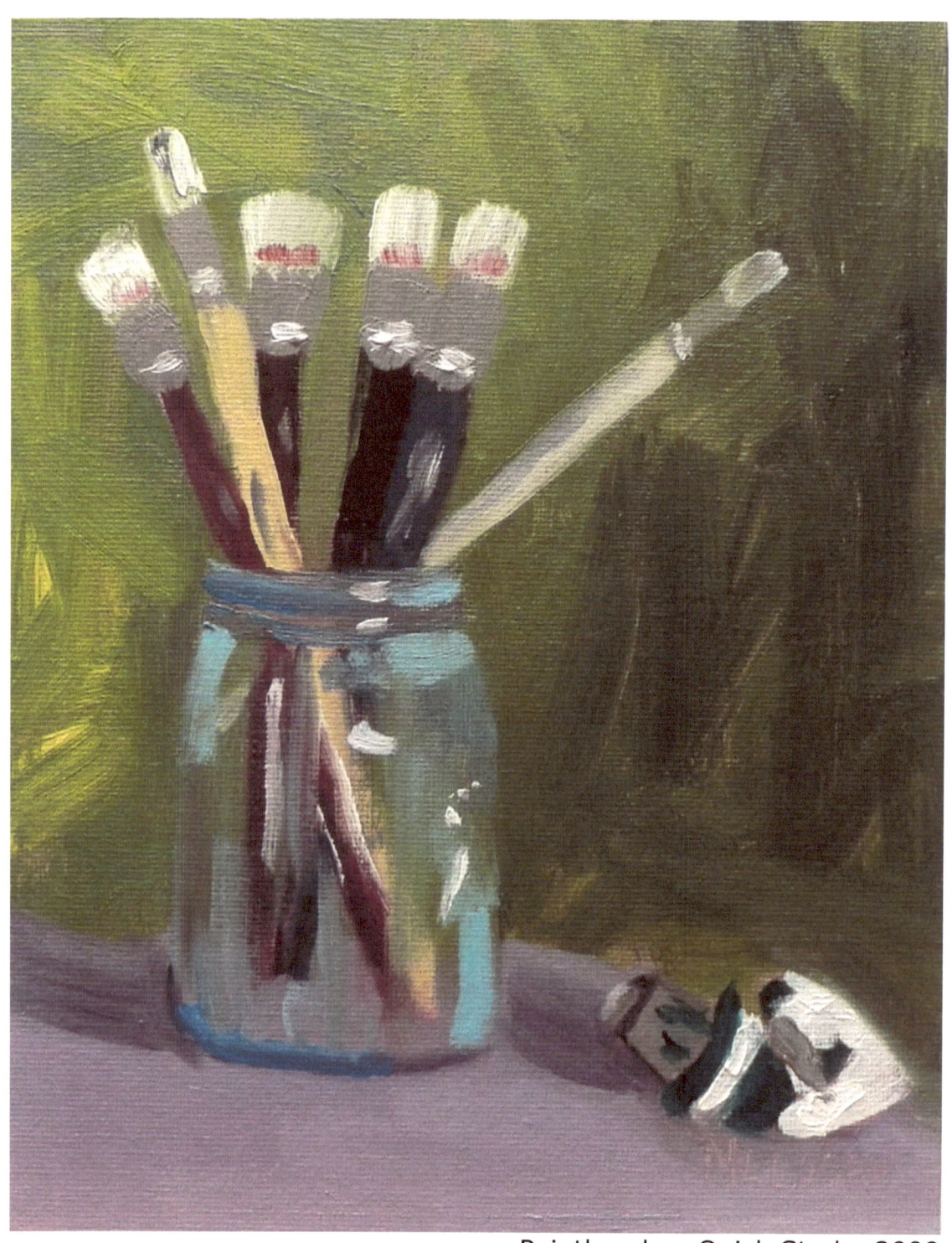

Paintbrushes Quick Study. 2009

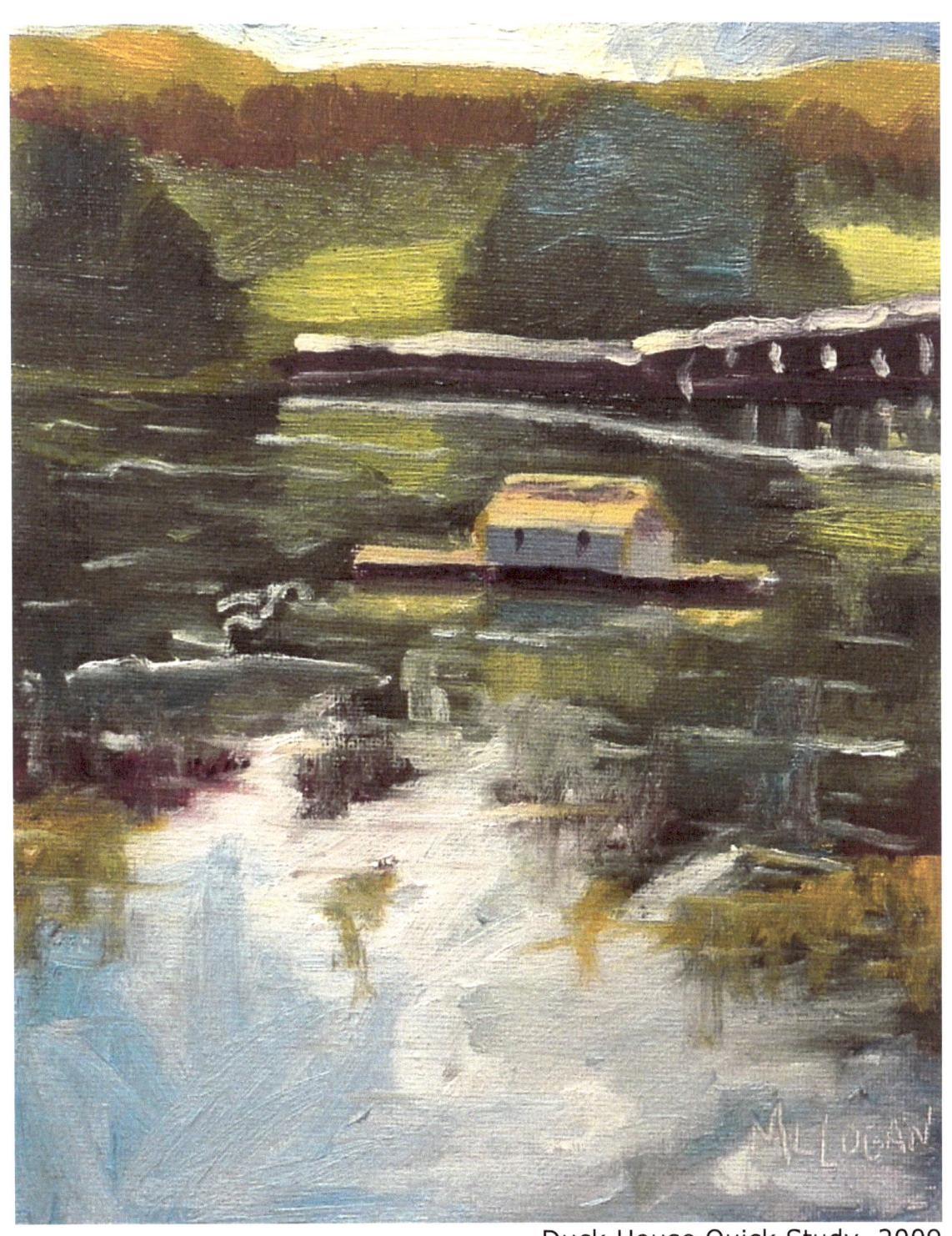

Duck House Quick Study, 2009

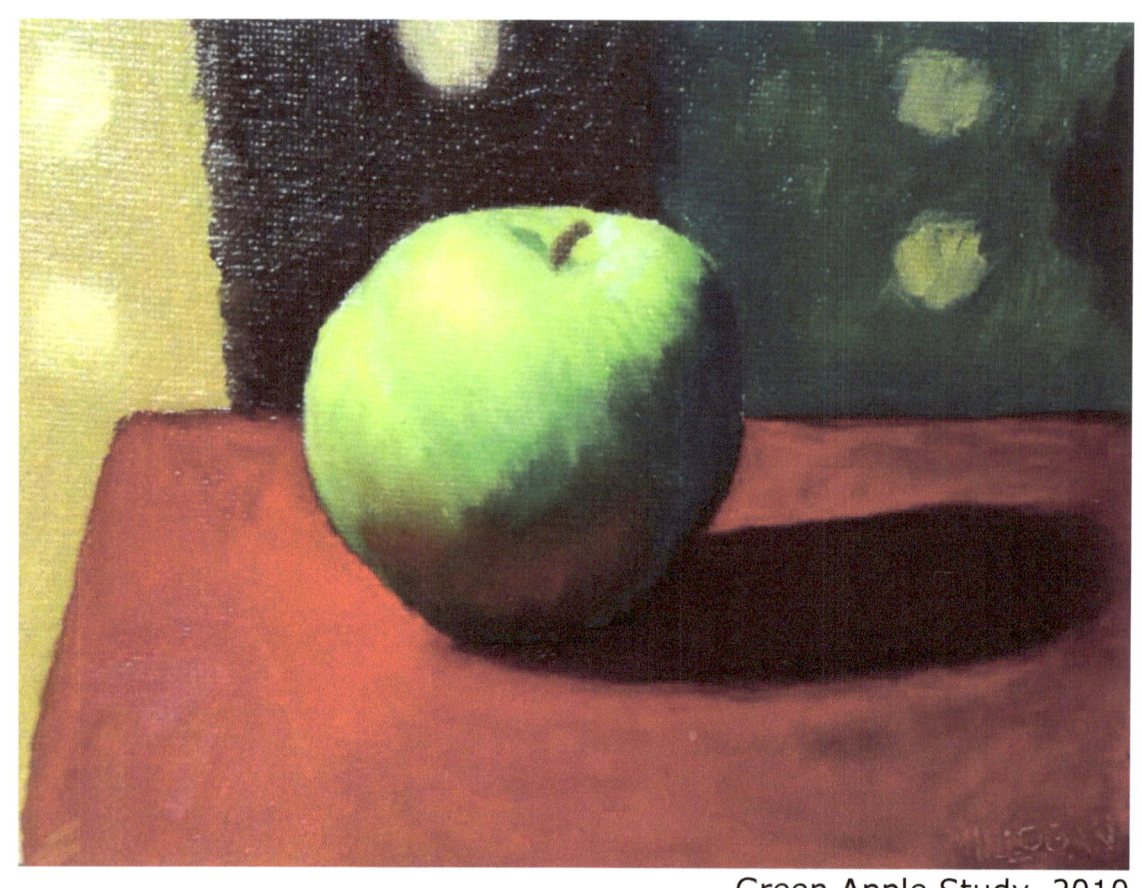

Green Apple Study, 2010

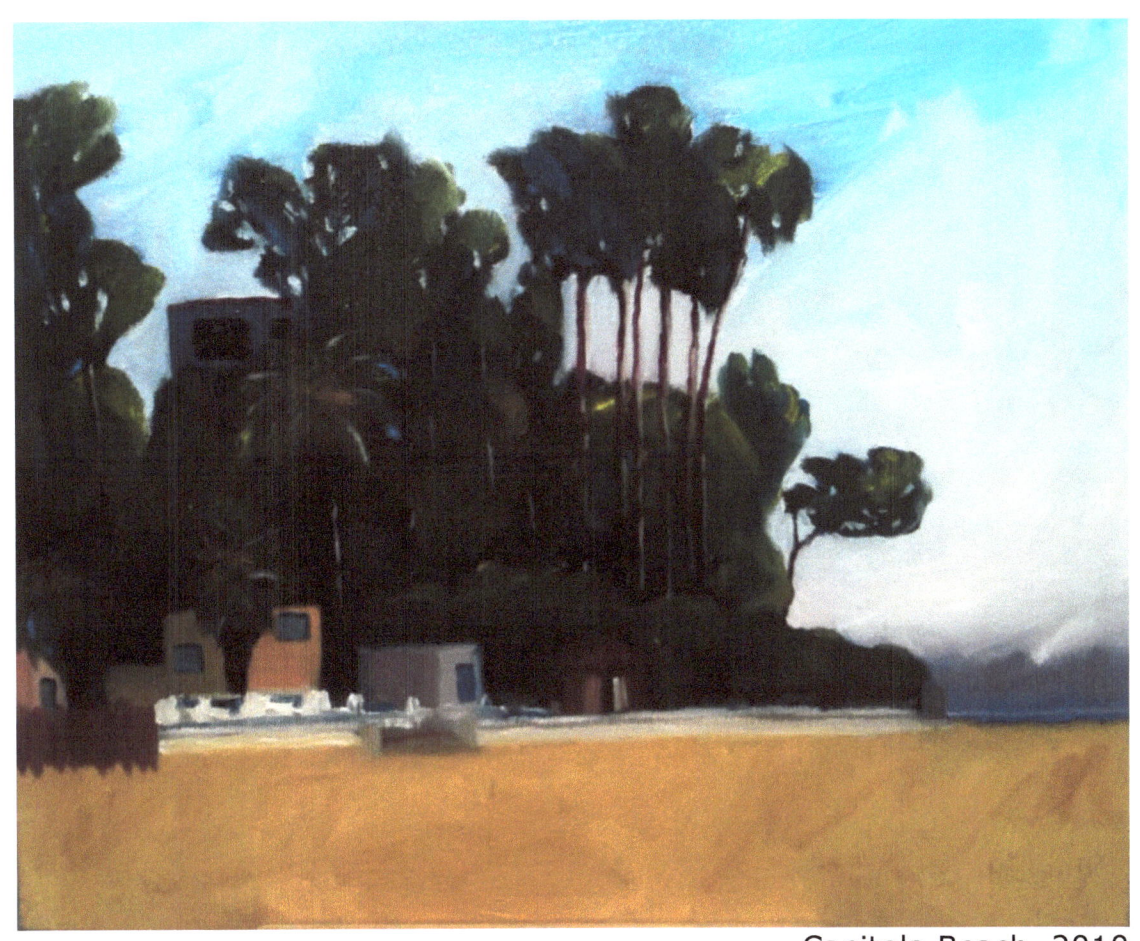

Capitola Beach, 2010

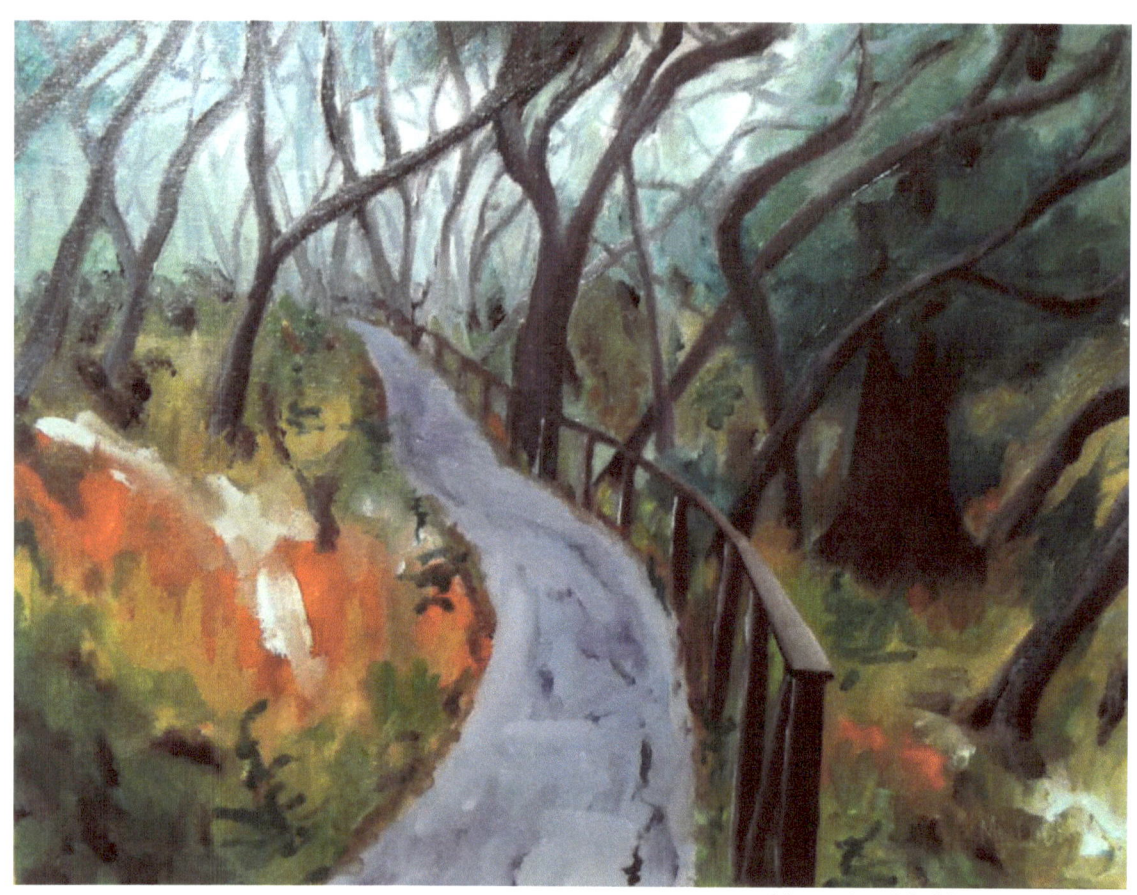

Kerr to McHenry, 2010

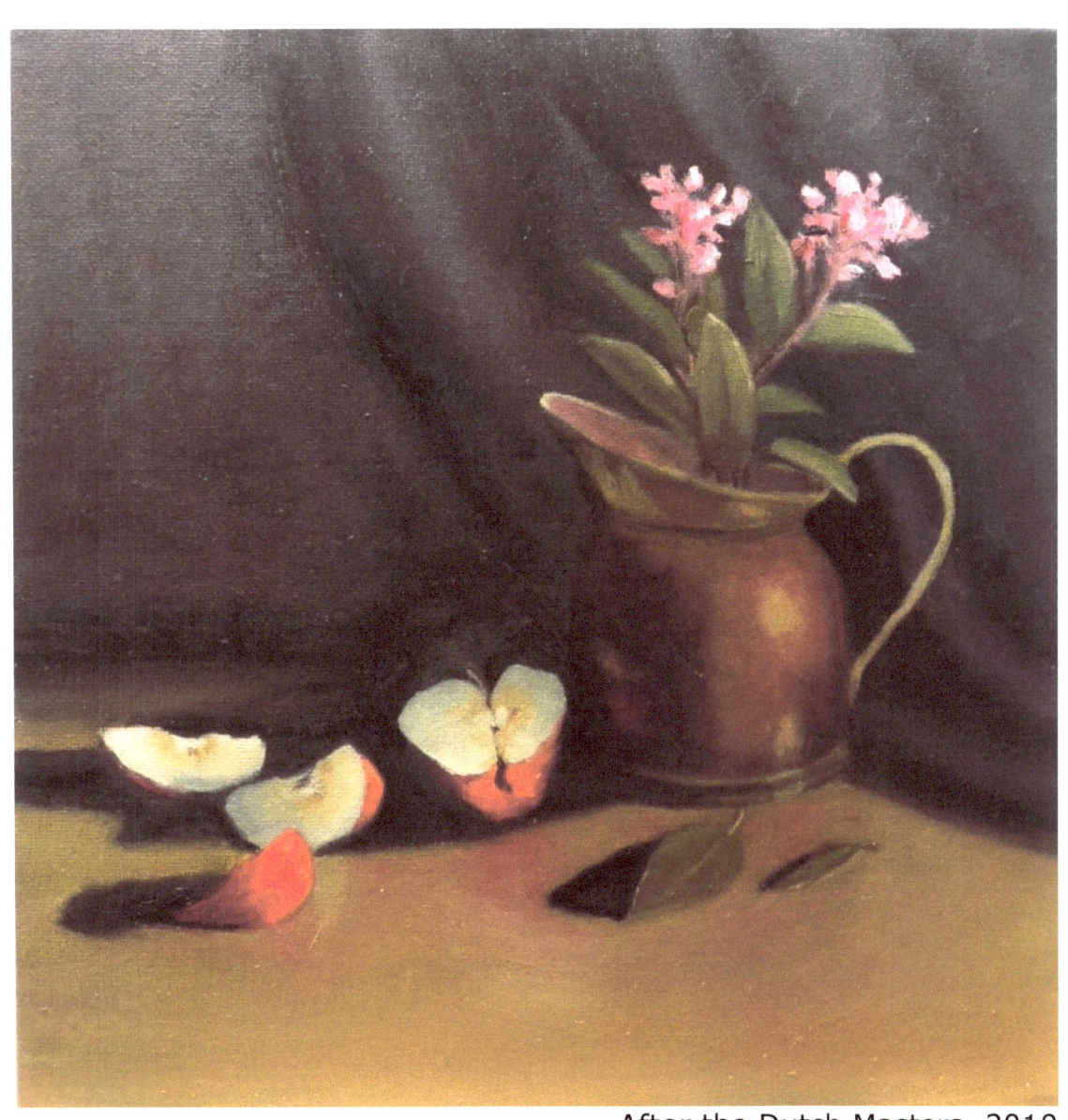

After the Dutch Masters, 2010

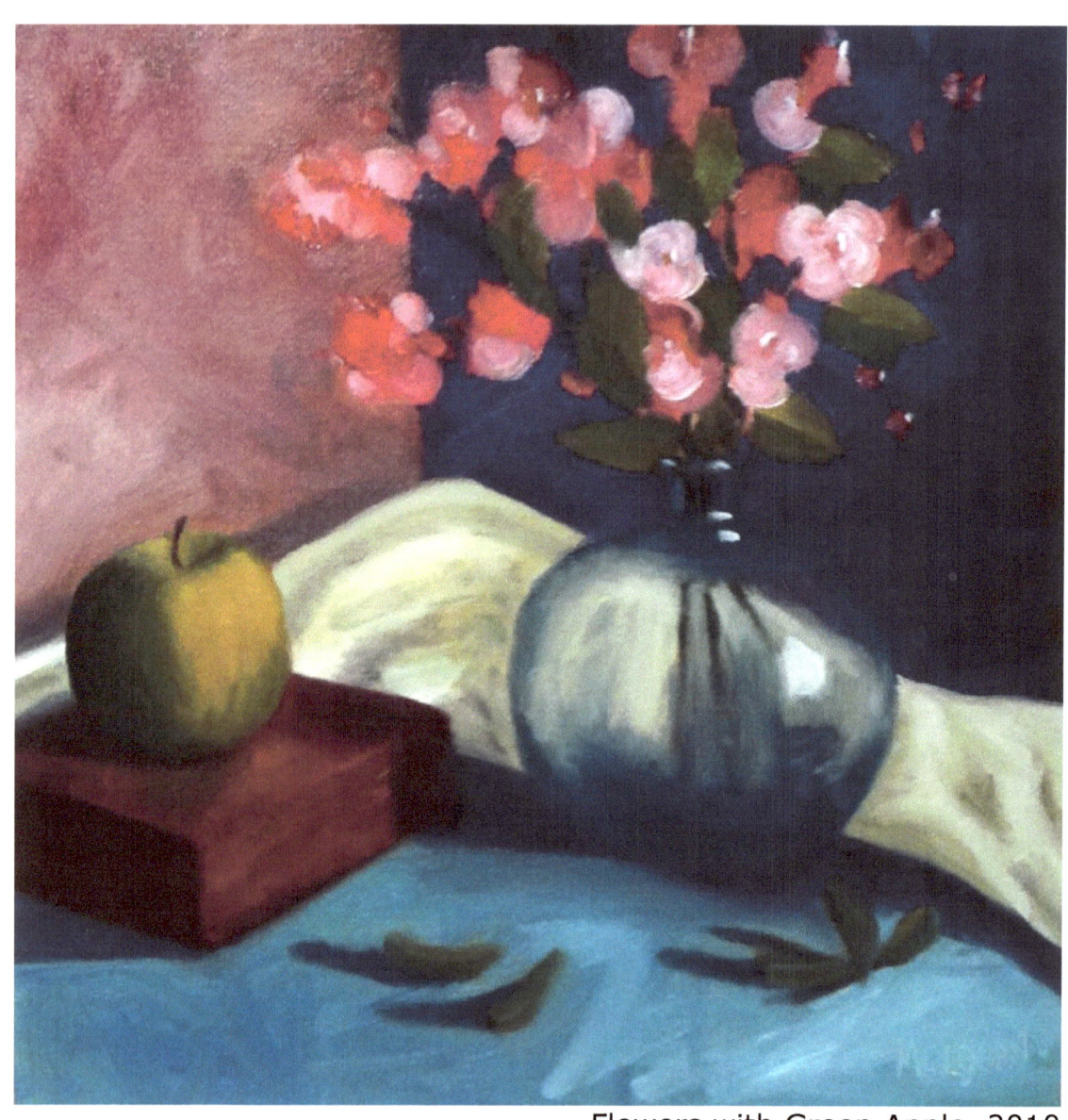

Flowers with Green Apple, 2010

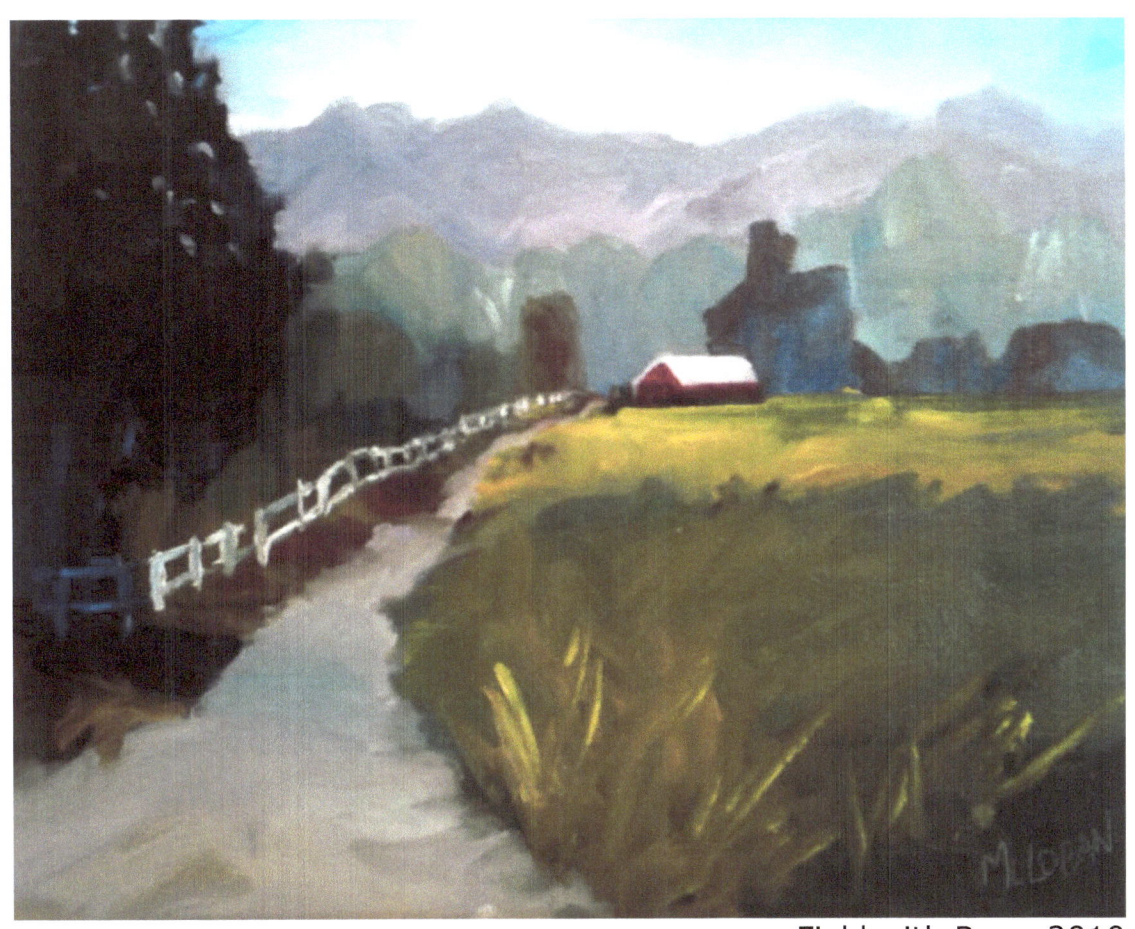

Field with Barn, 2010

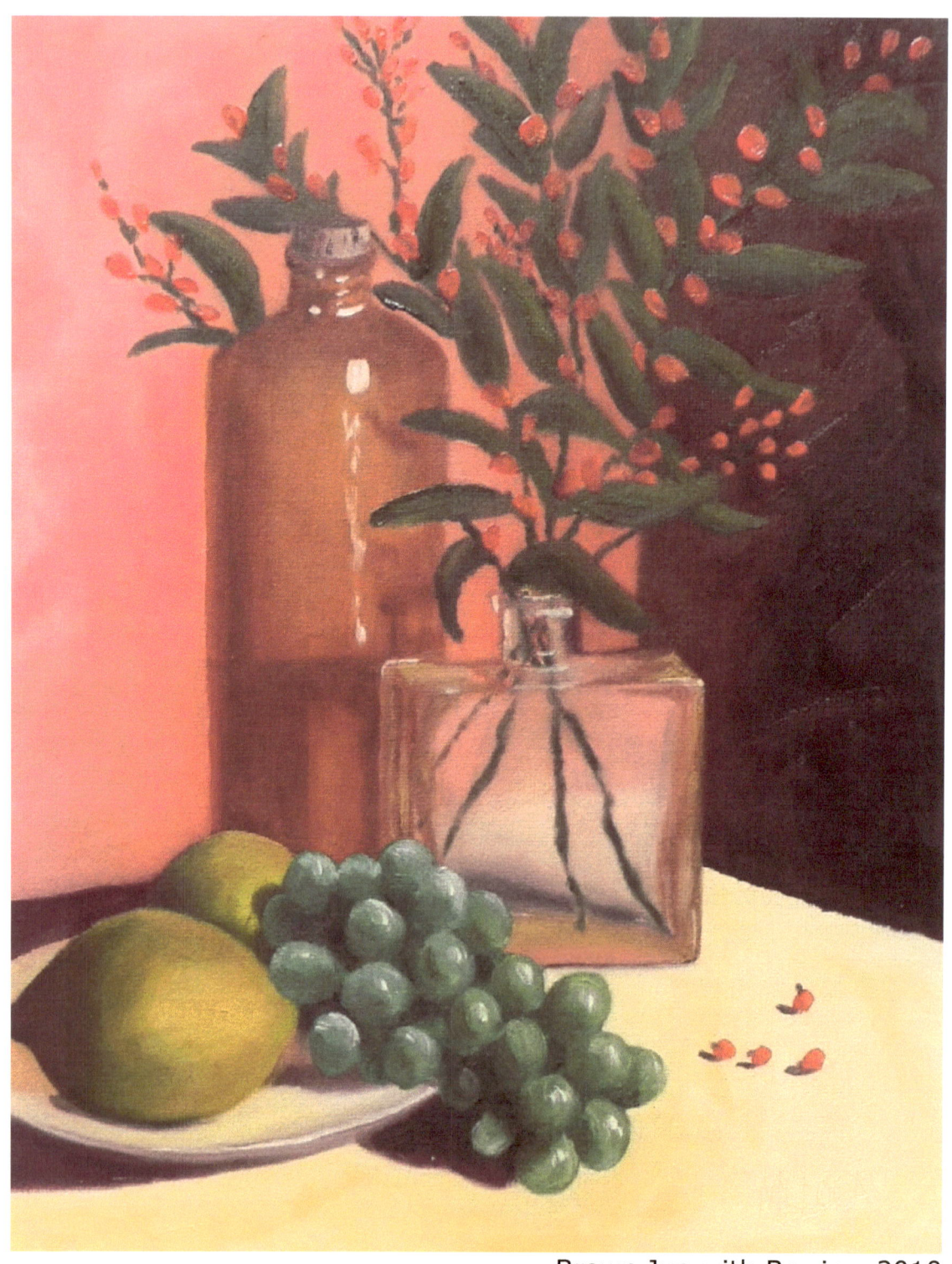

Brown Jug with Berries, 2010

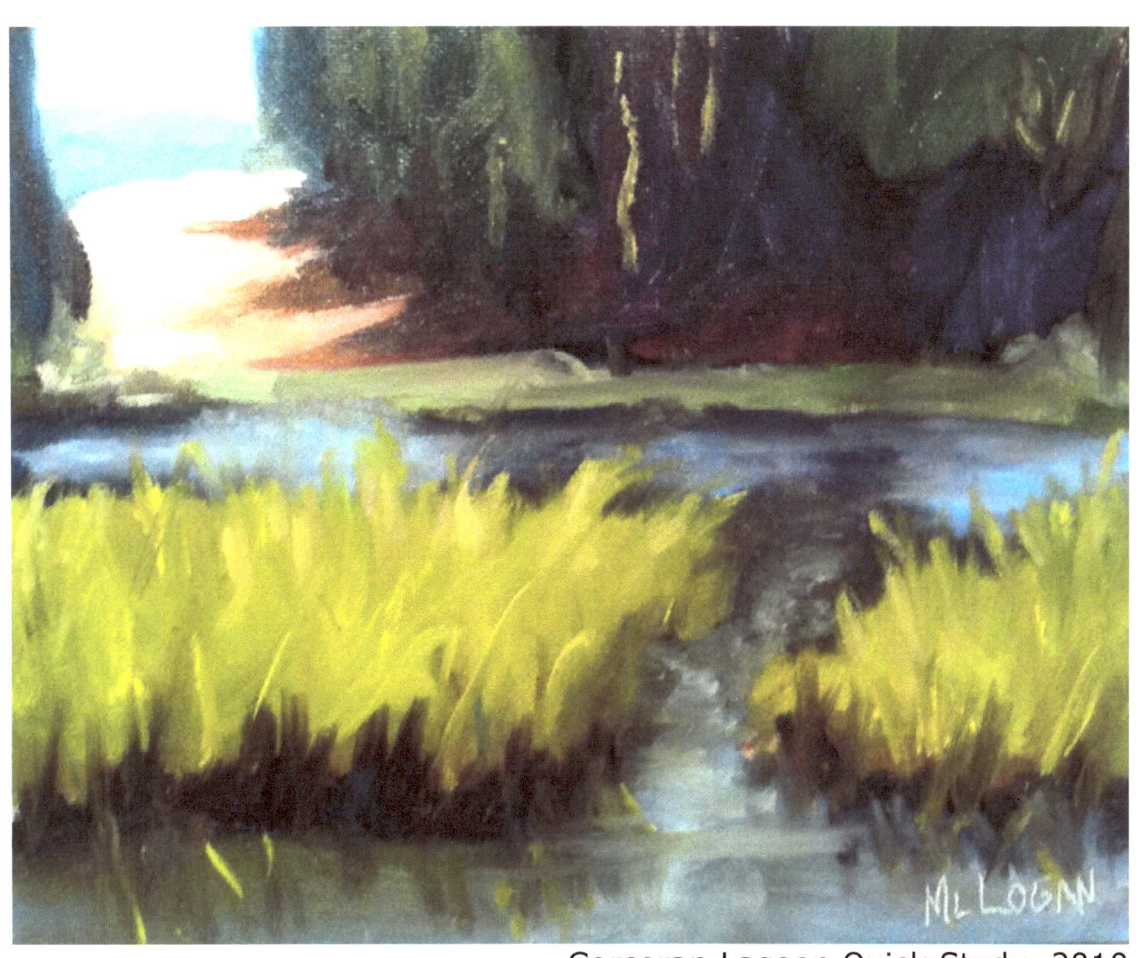

Corcoran Lagoon Quick Study, 2010

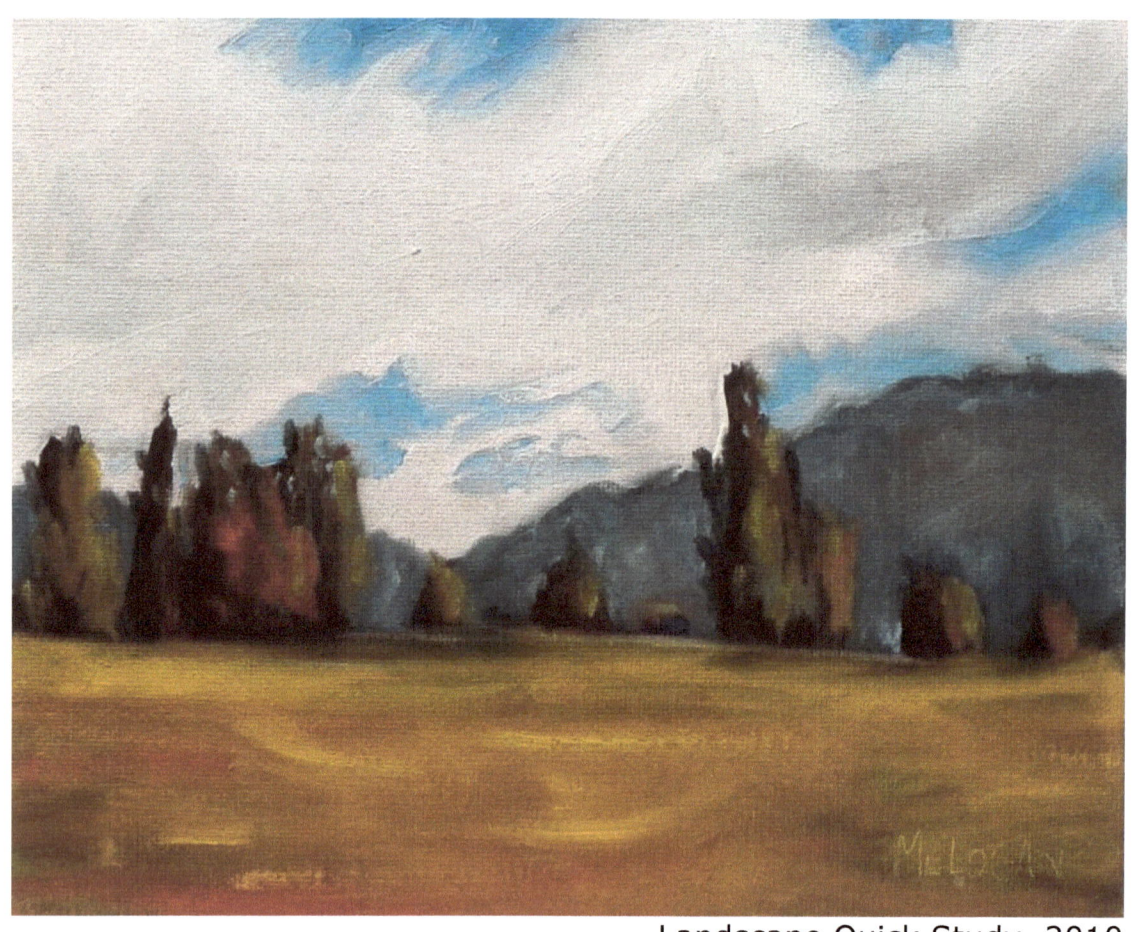

Landscape Quick Study, 2010

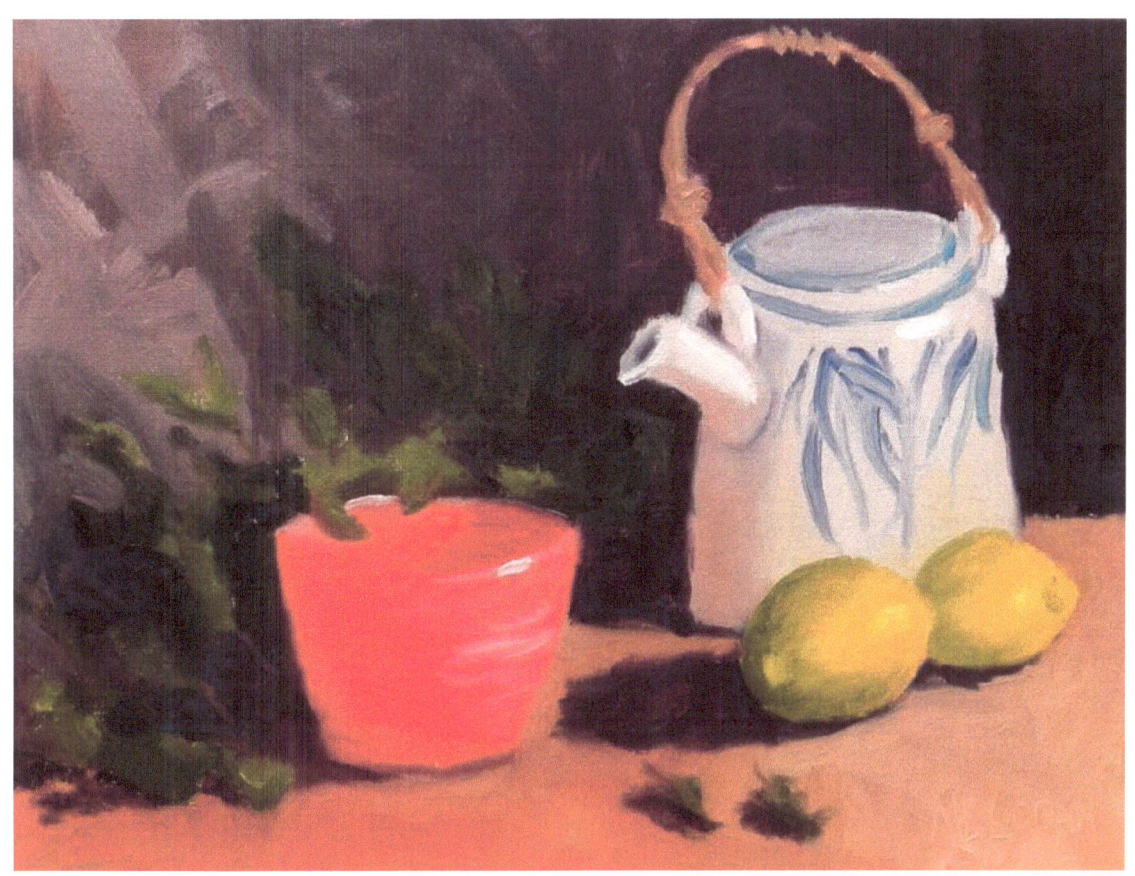

Teapot with Red Bowl, 2010

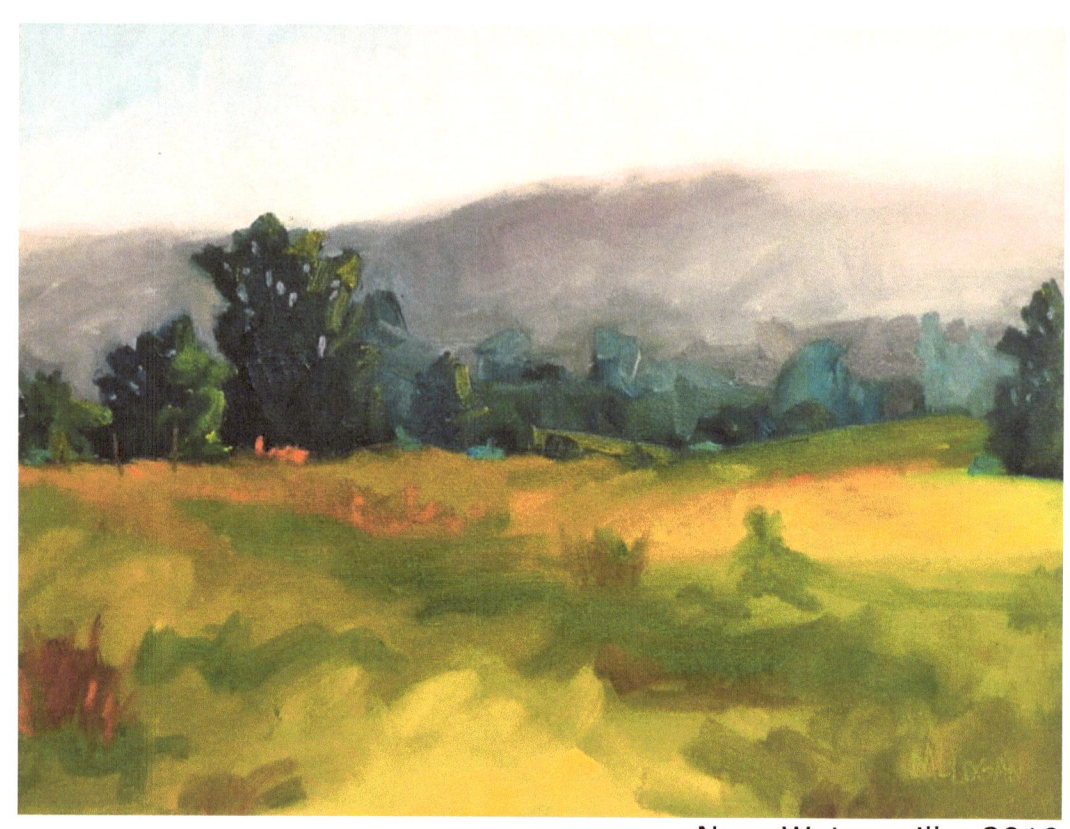

Near Watsonville, 2010

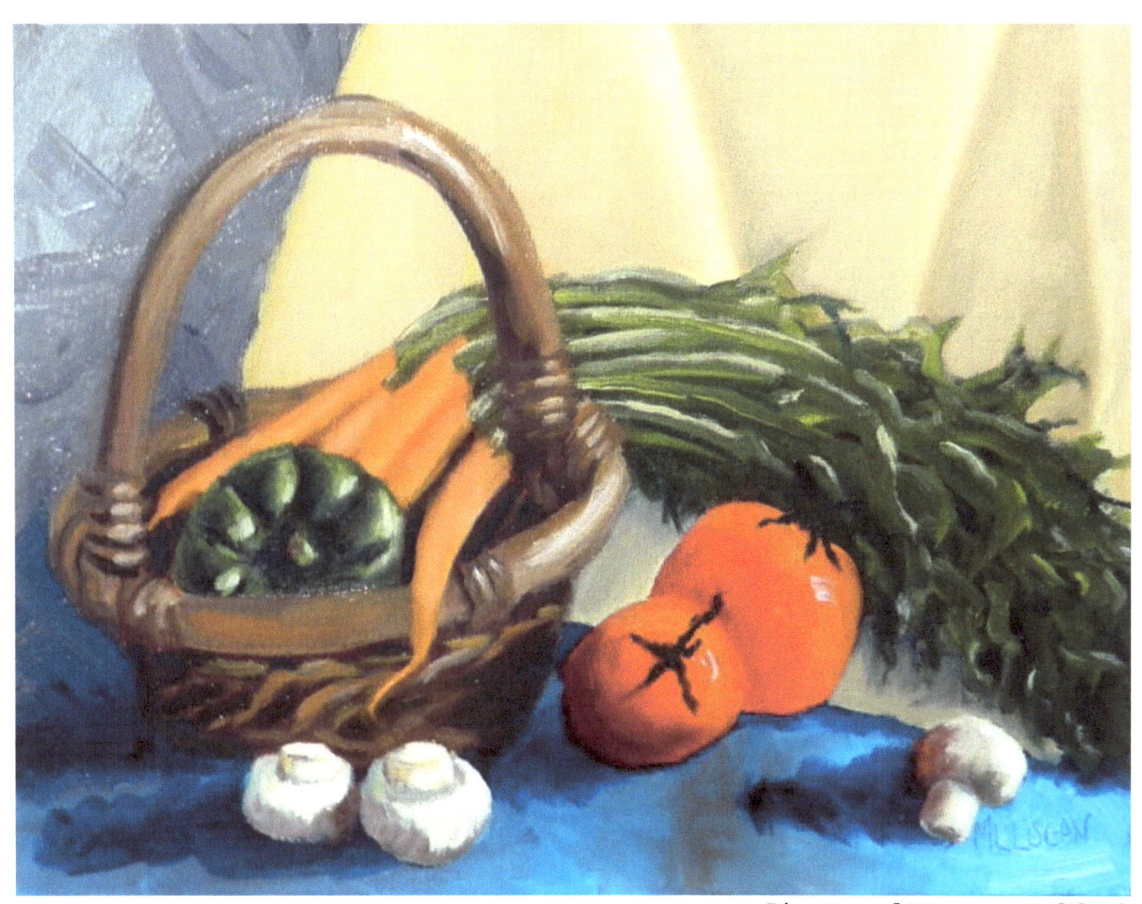

Plenty of Veggies, 2010

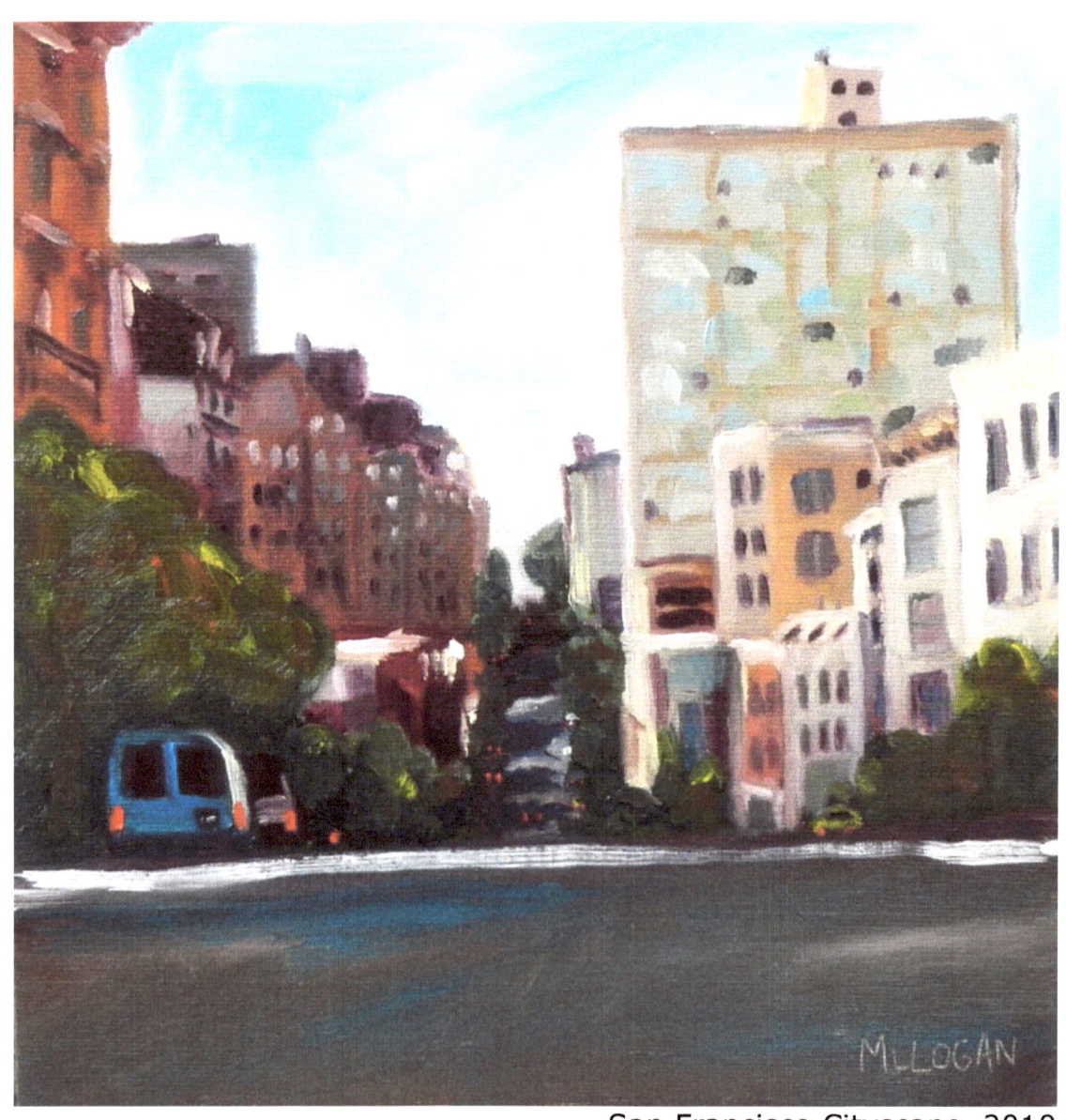

San Francisco Cityscape, 2010

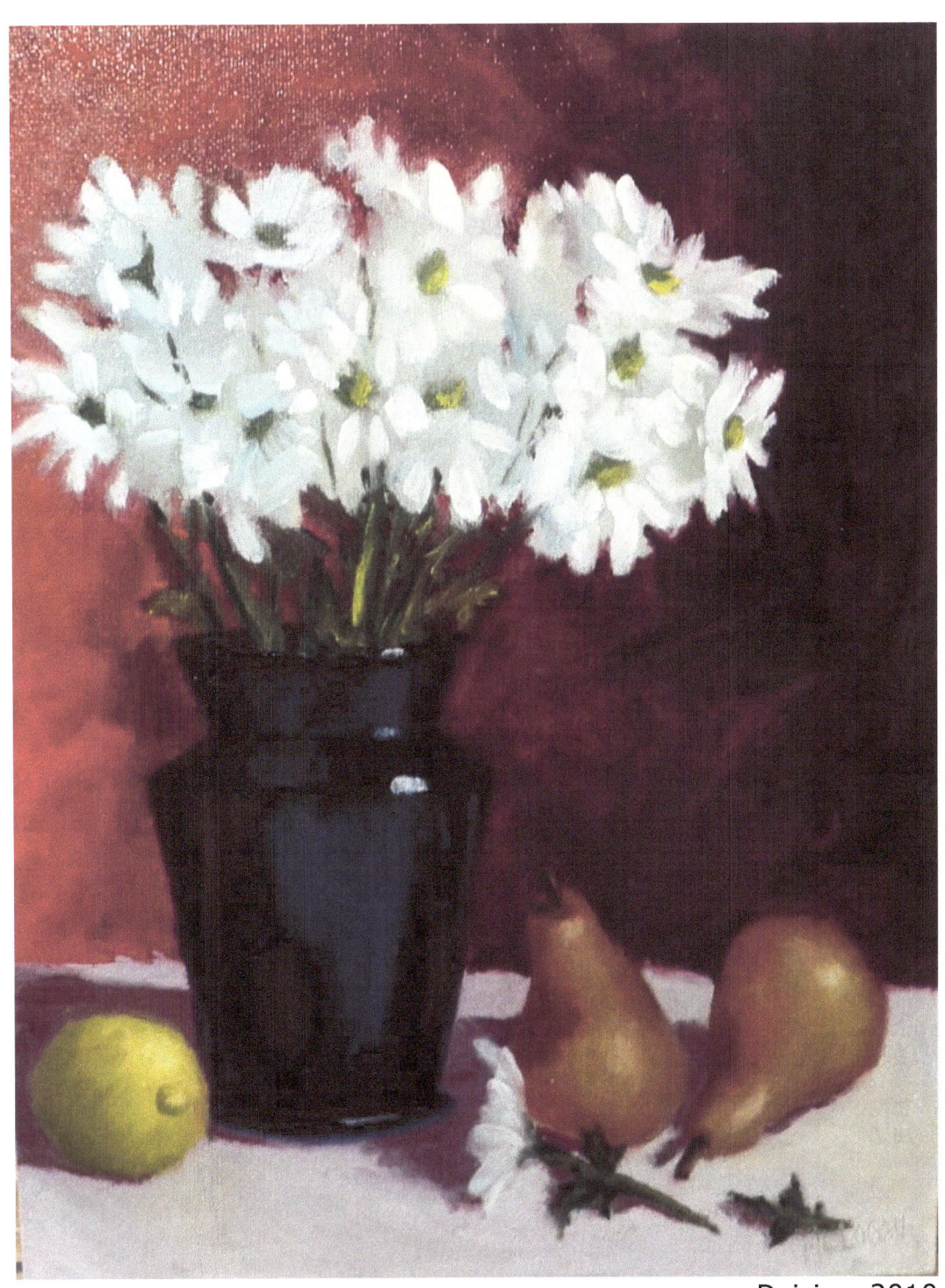

Daisies, 2010

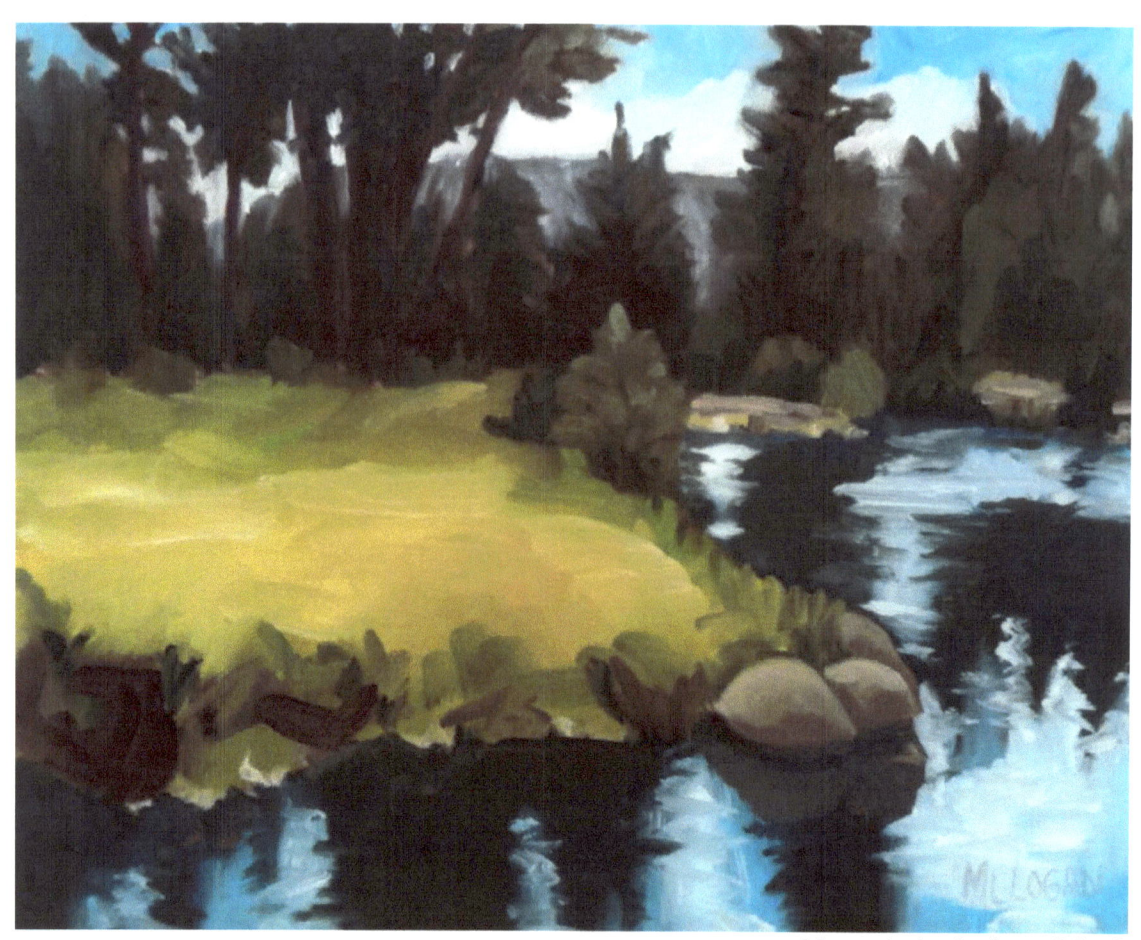

Mountain Lake, 2010

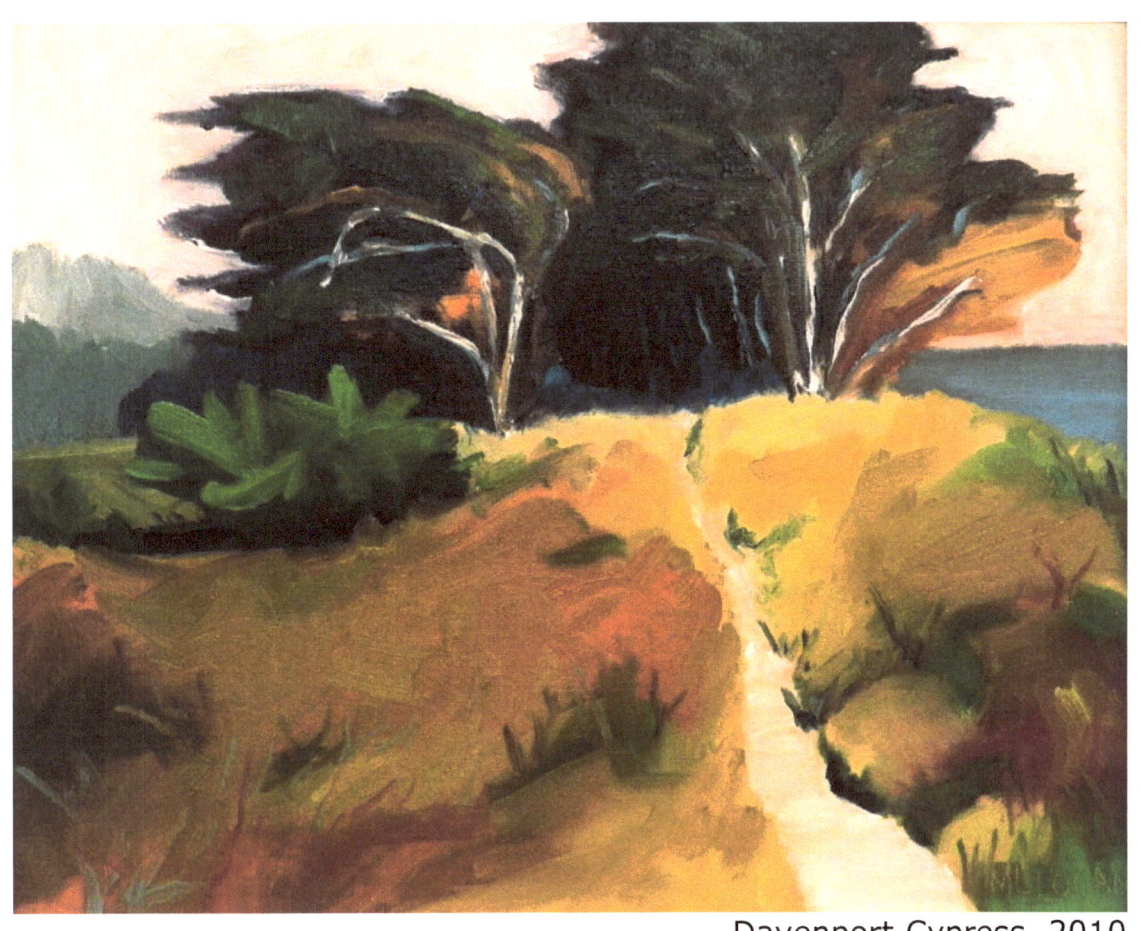
Davenport Cypress, 2010

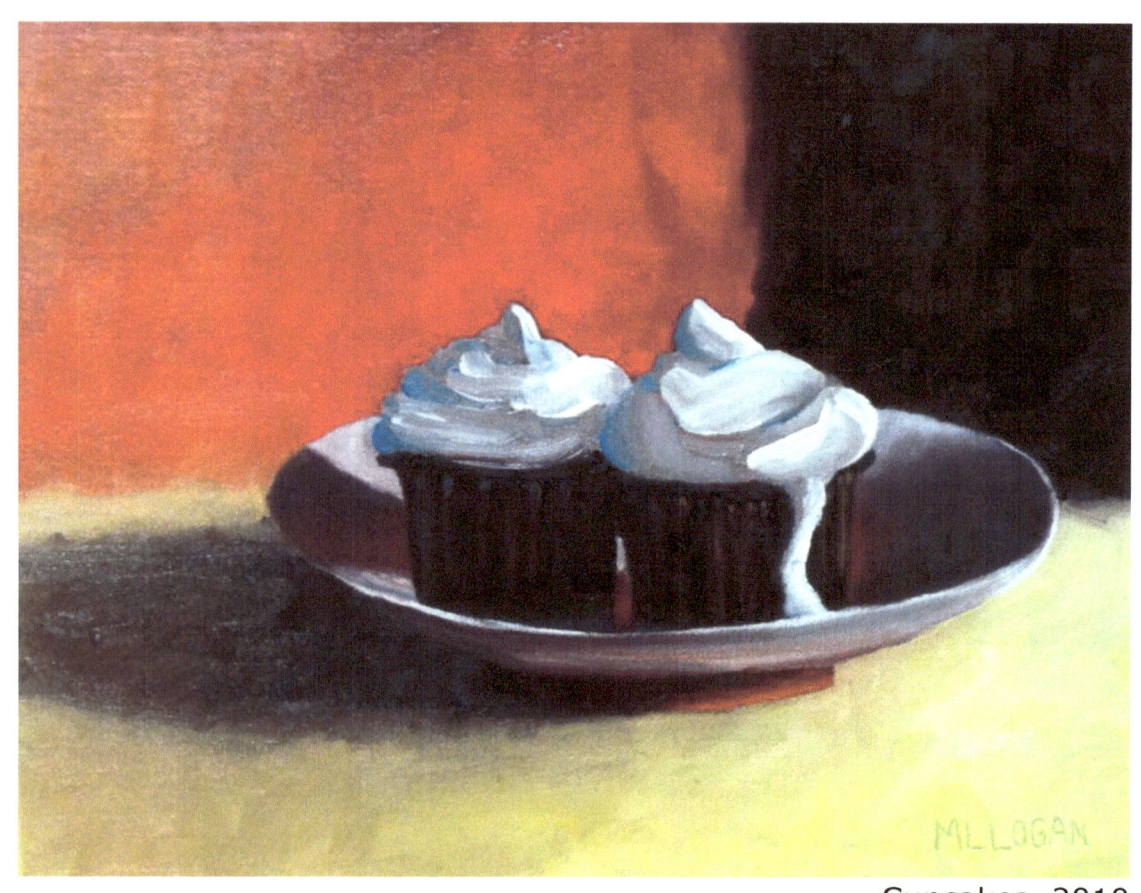

Cupcakes, 2010

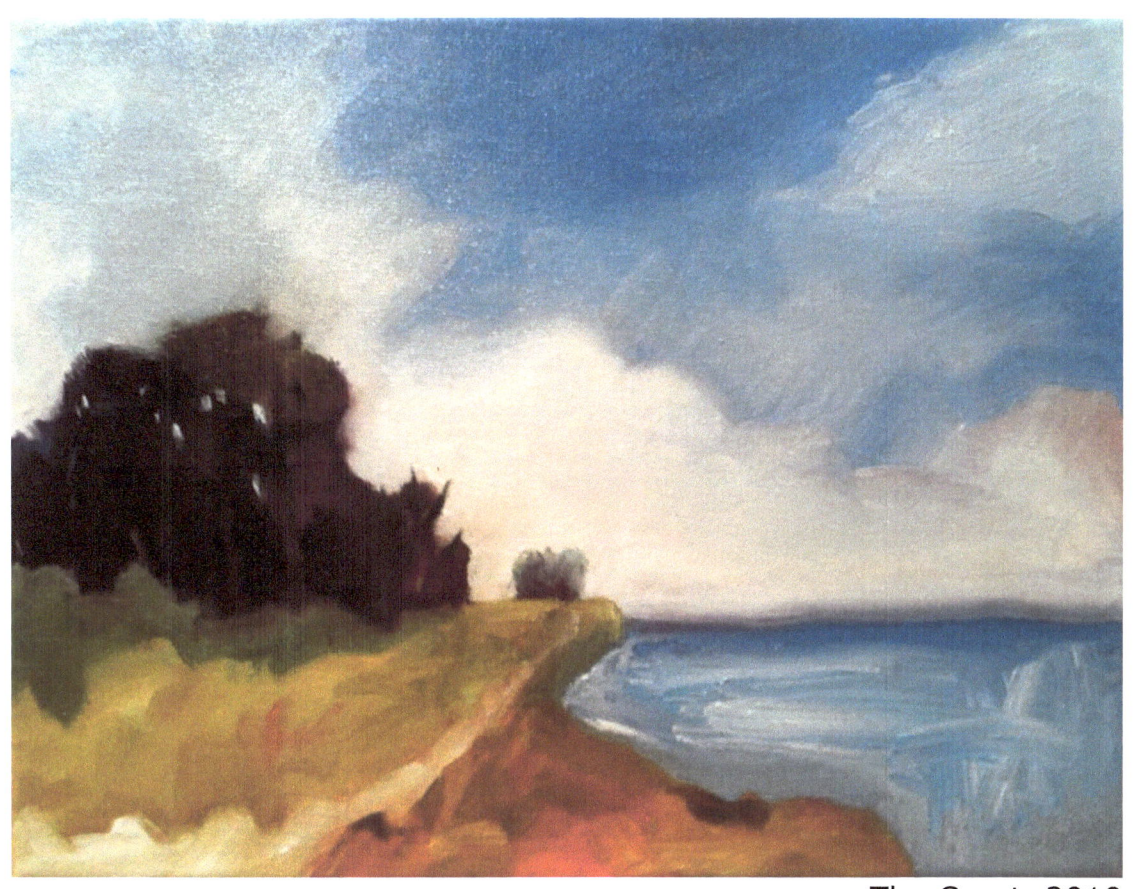

The Coast, 2010

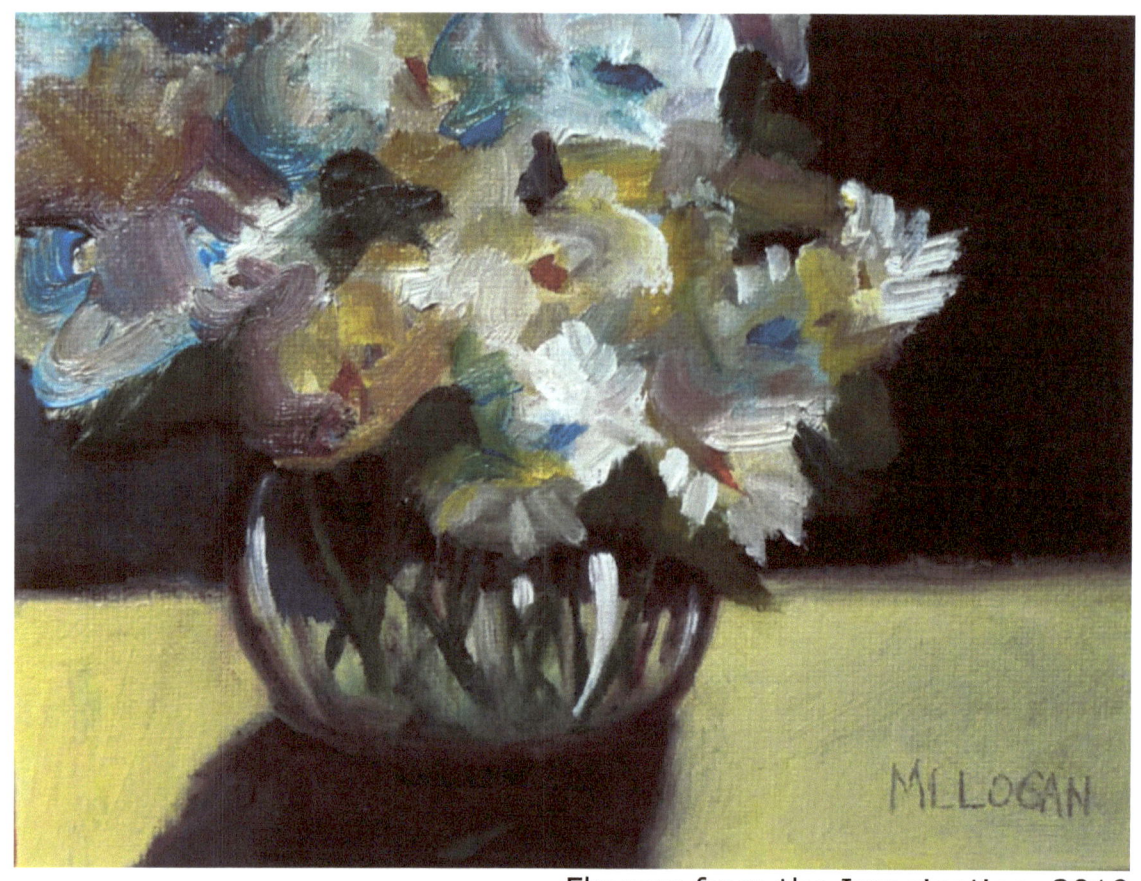

Flowers from the Imagination, 2010

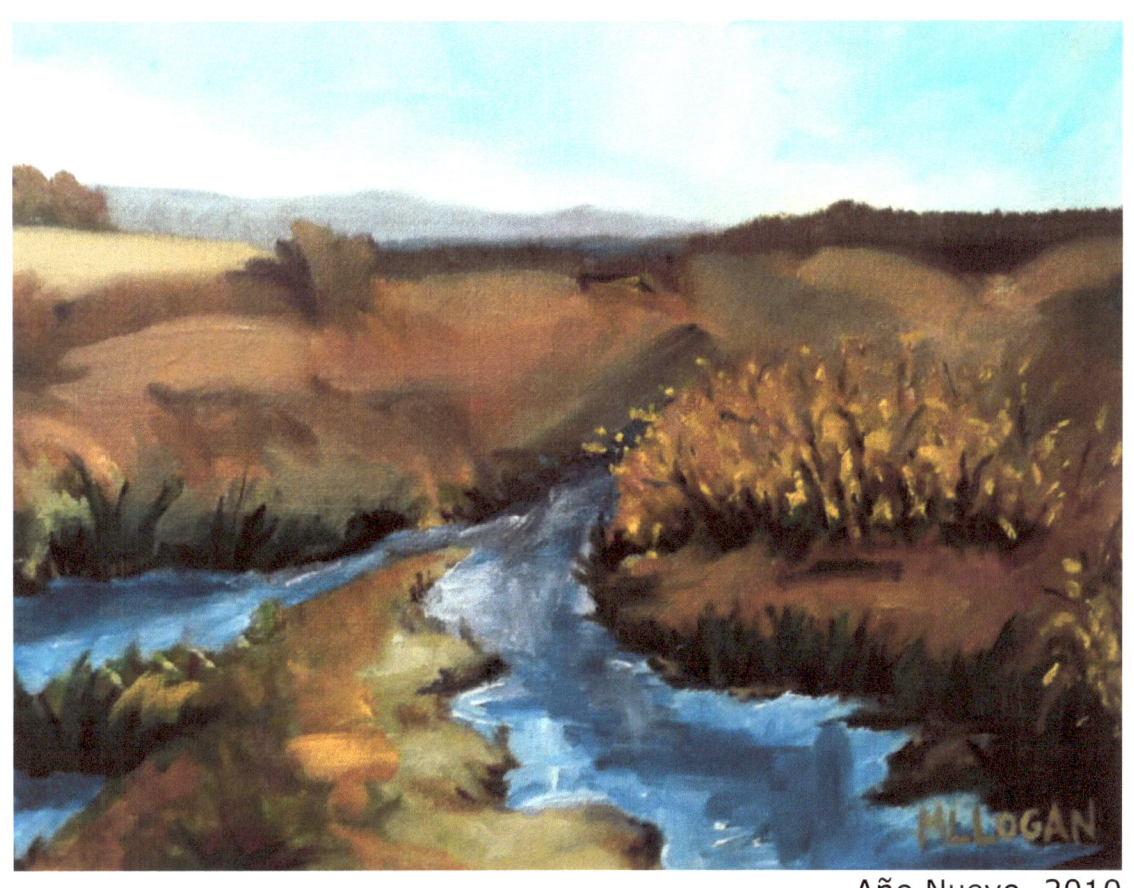

Año Nuevo, 2010

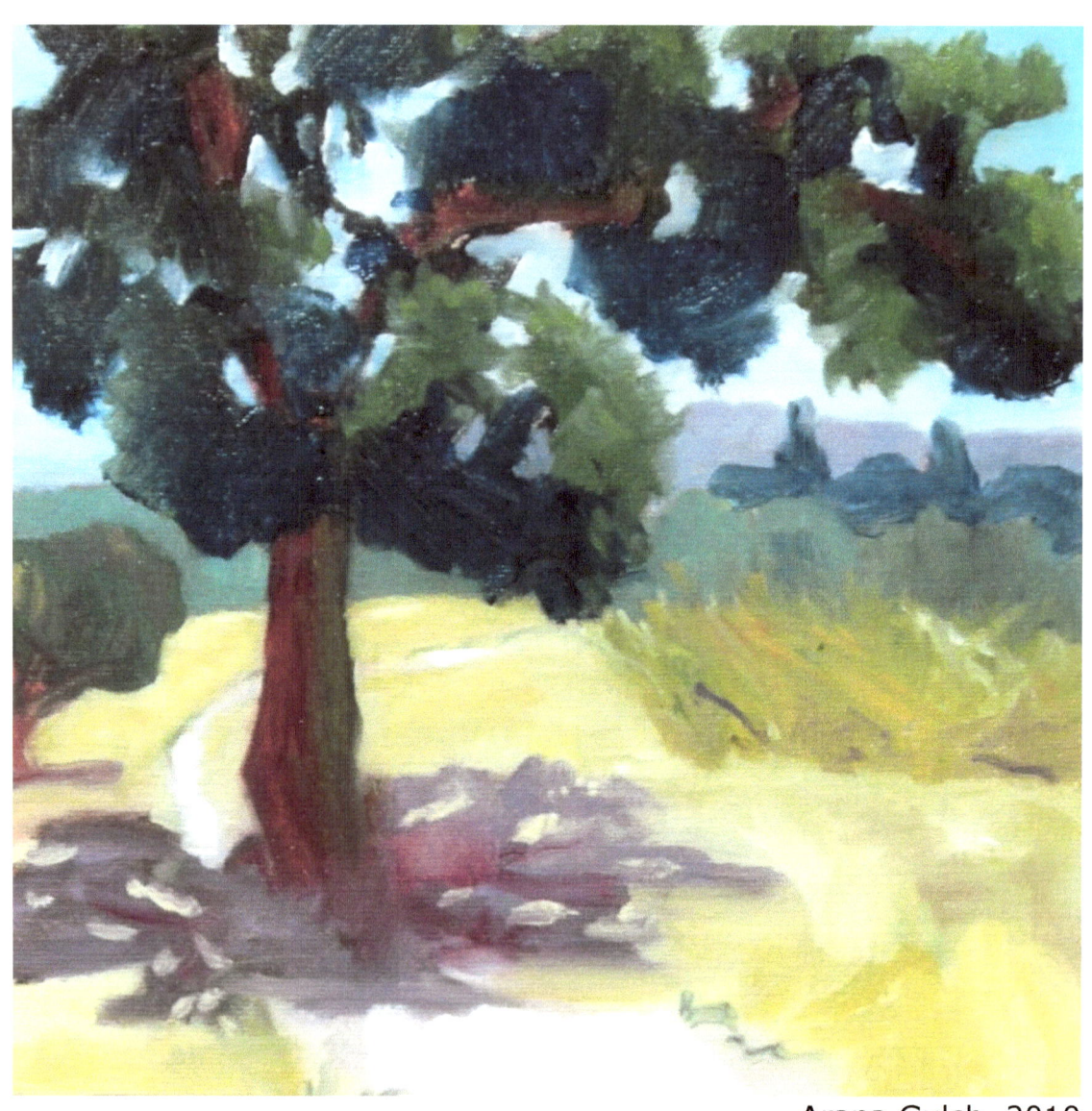

Arana Gulch, 2010

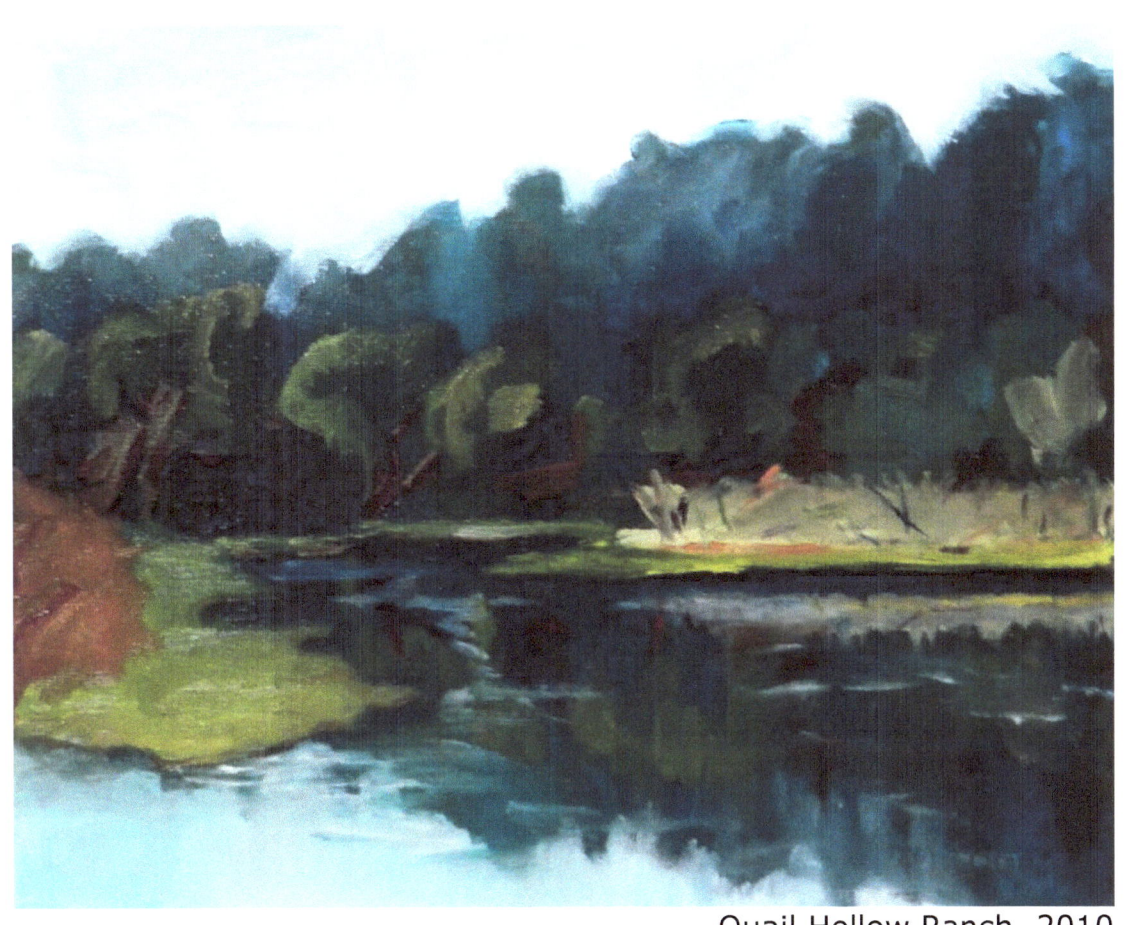

Quail Hollow Ranch, 2010

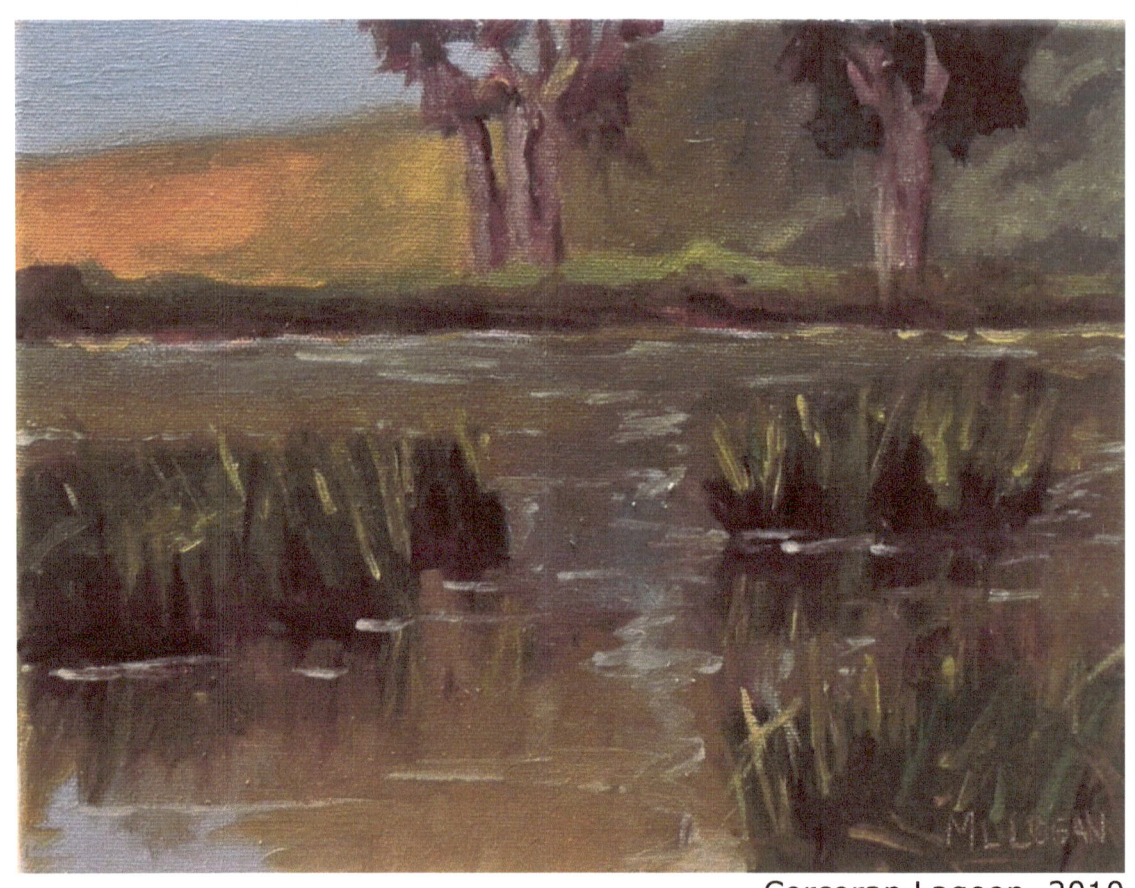

Corcoran Lagoon, 2010

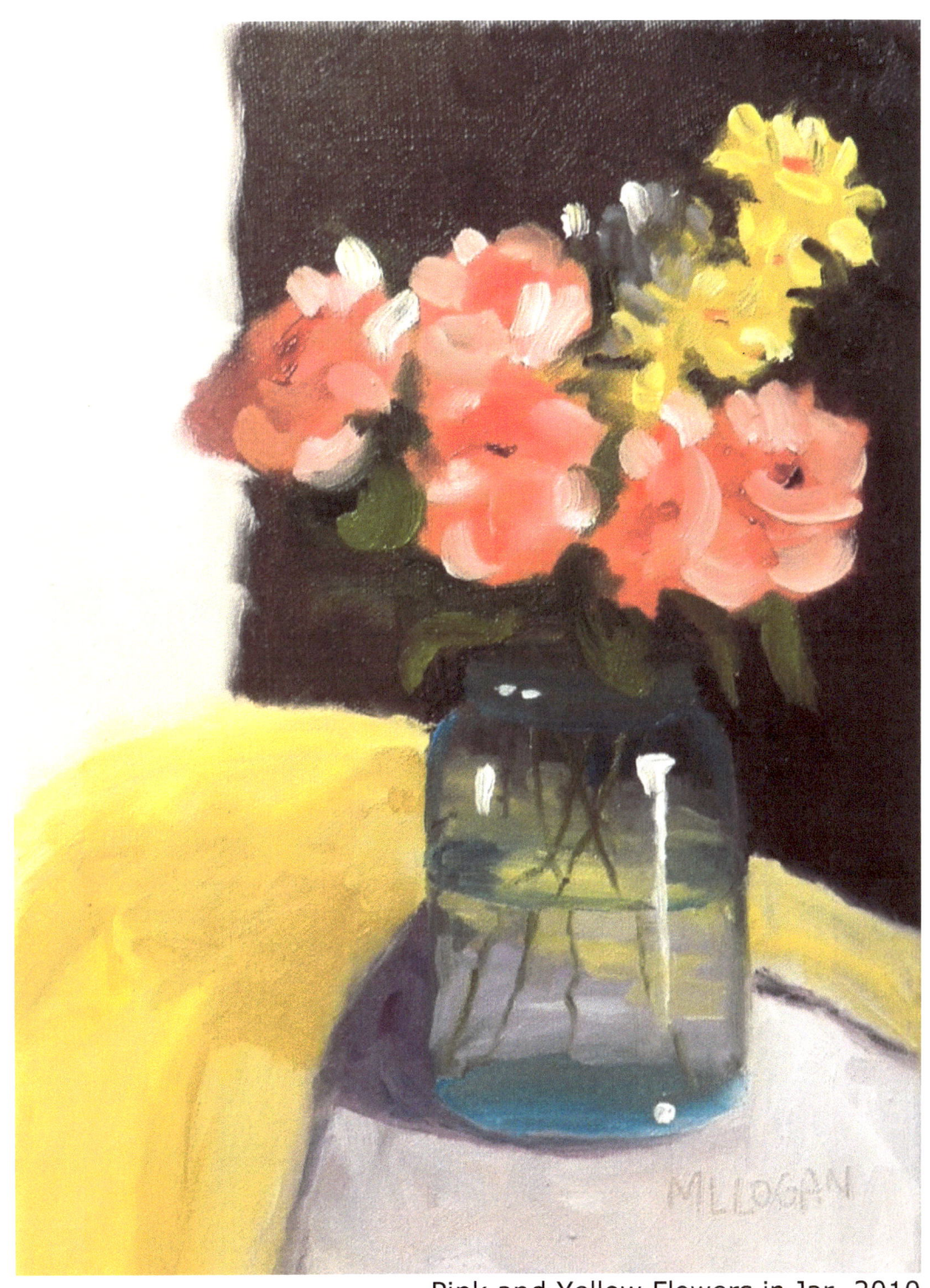

Pink and Yellow Flowers in Jar, 2010

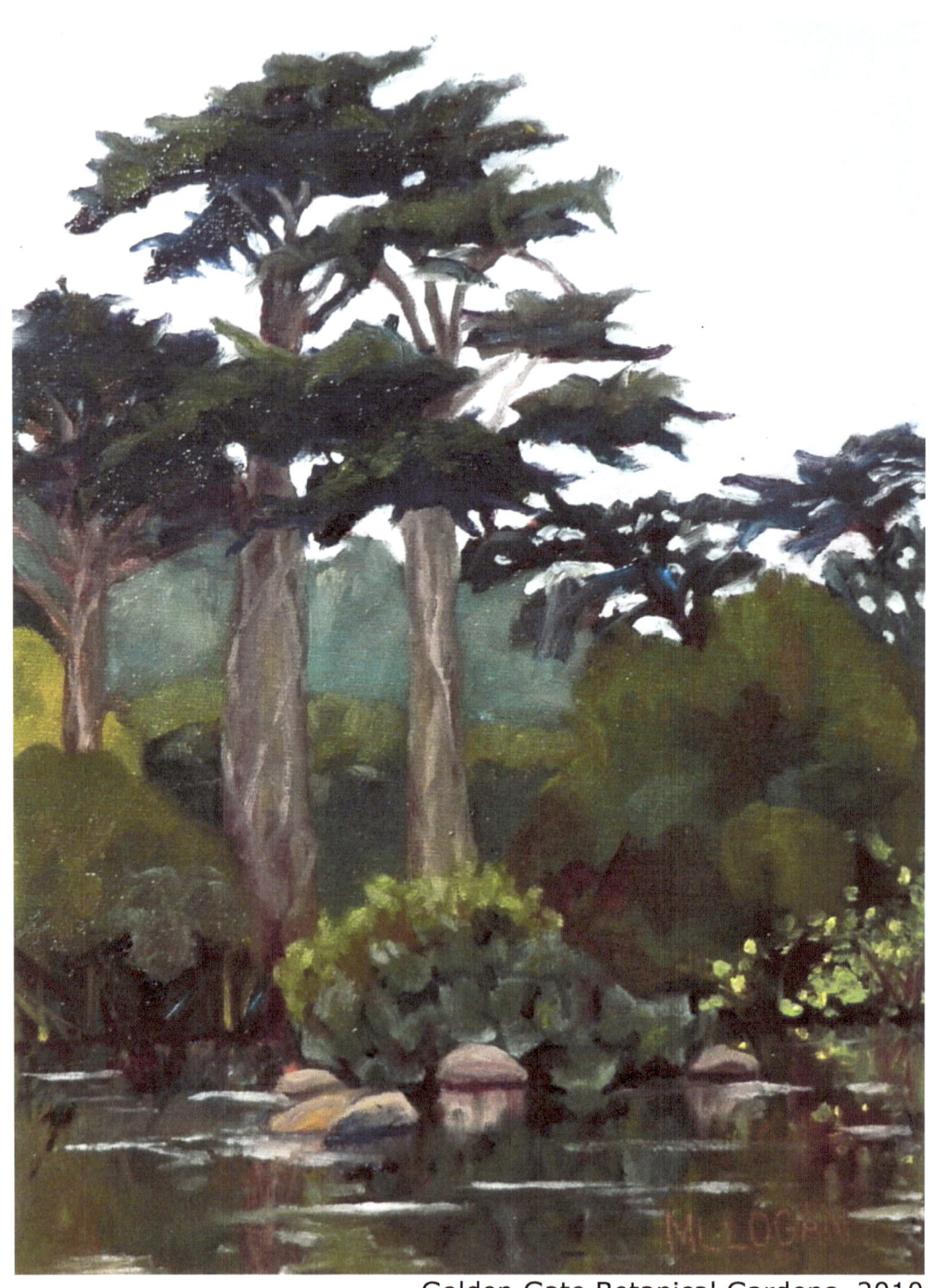

Golden Gate Botanical Gardens, 2010

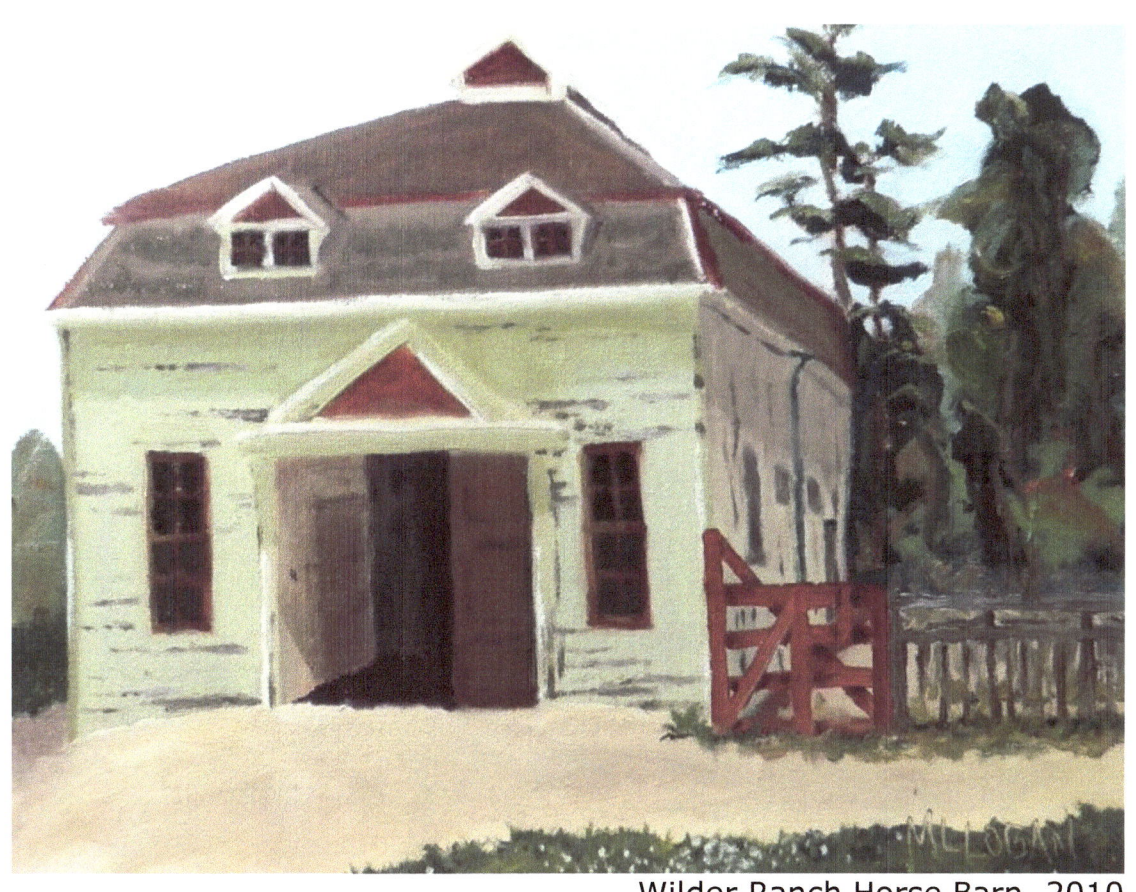

Wilder Ranch Horse Barn, 2010

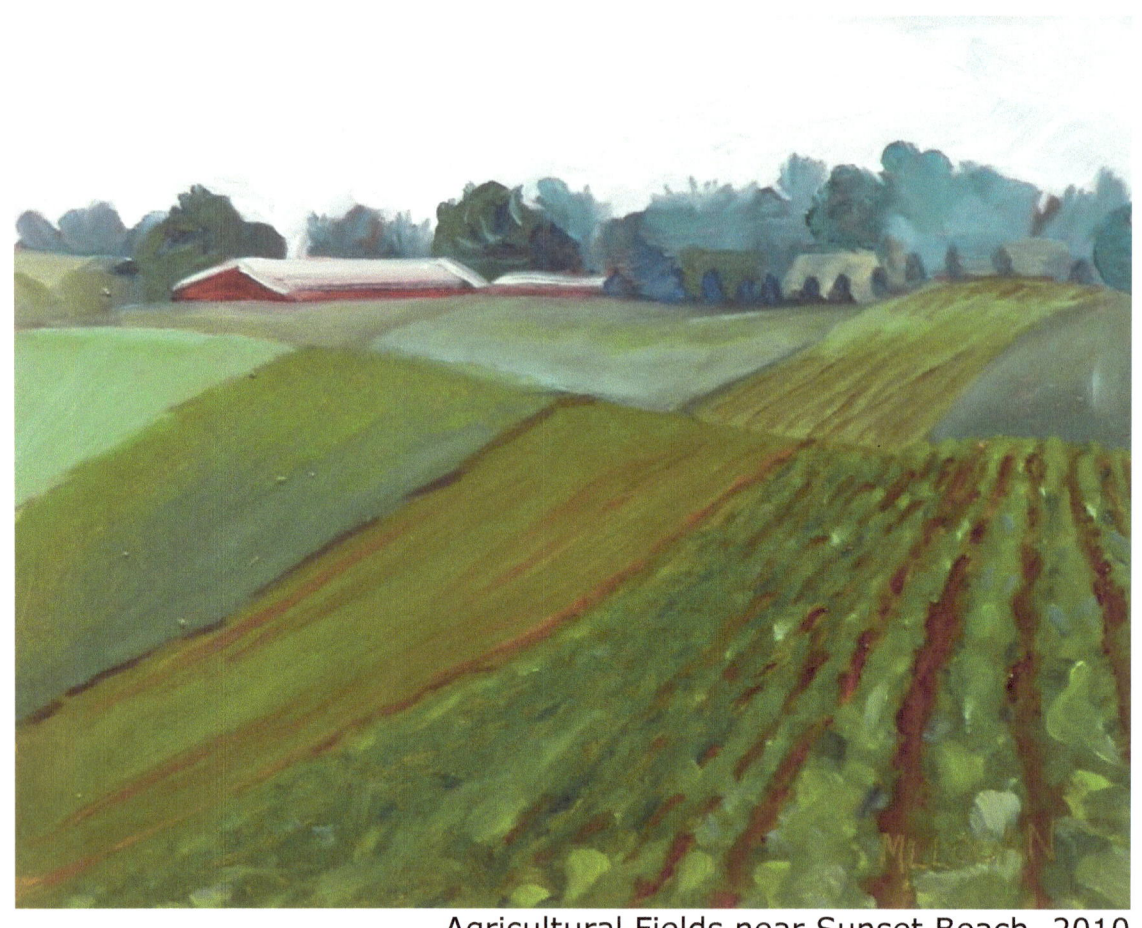

Agricultural Fields near Sunset Beach, 2010

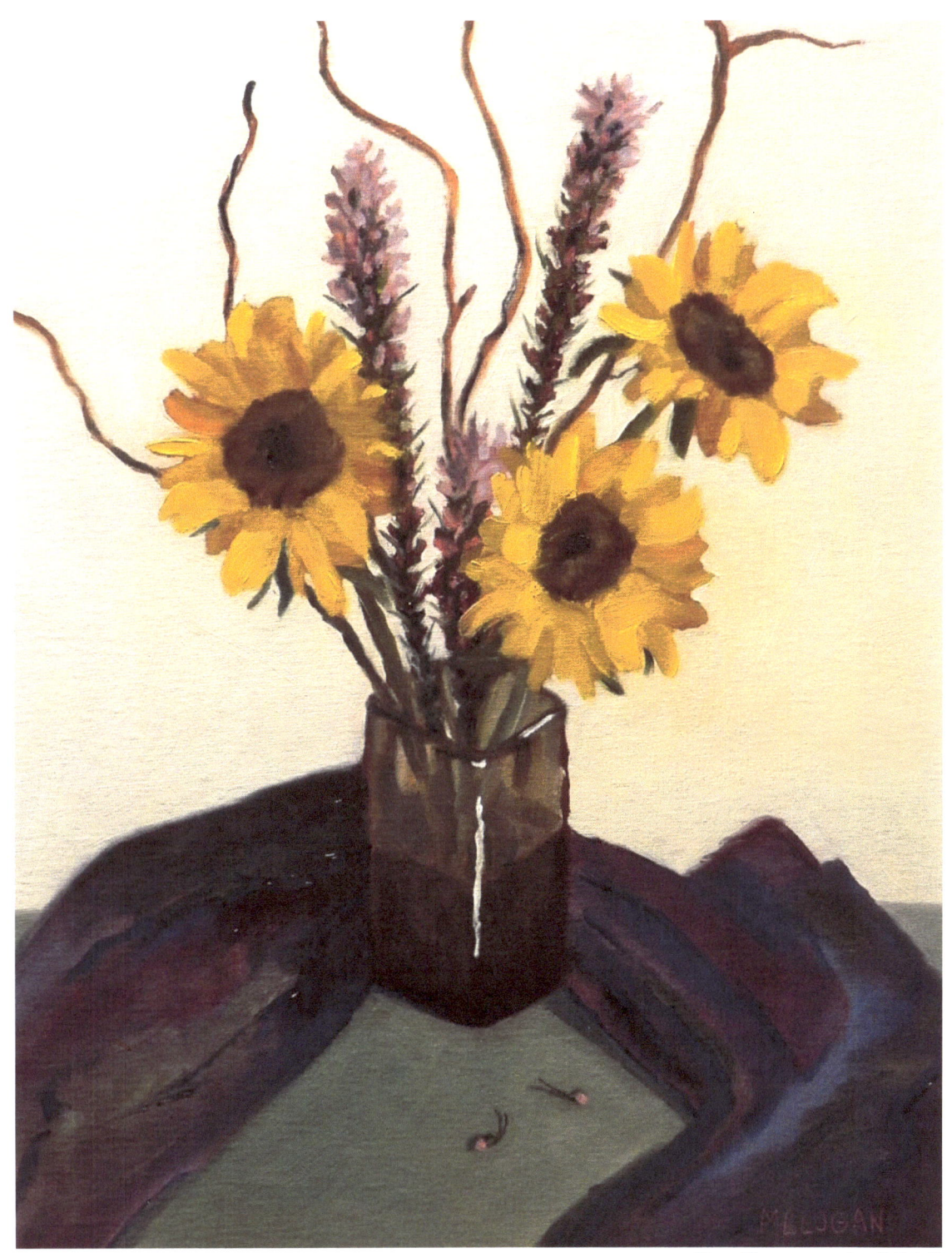

Sunflowers 1, 2010

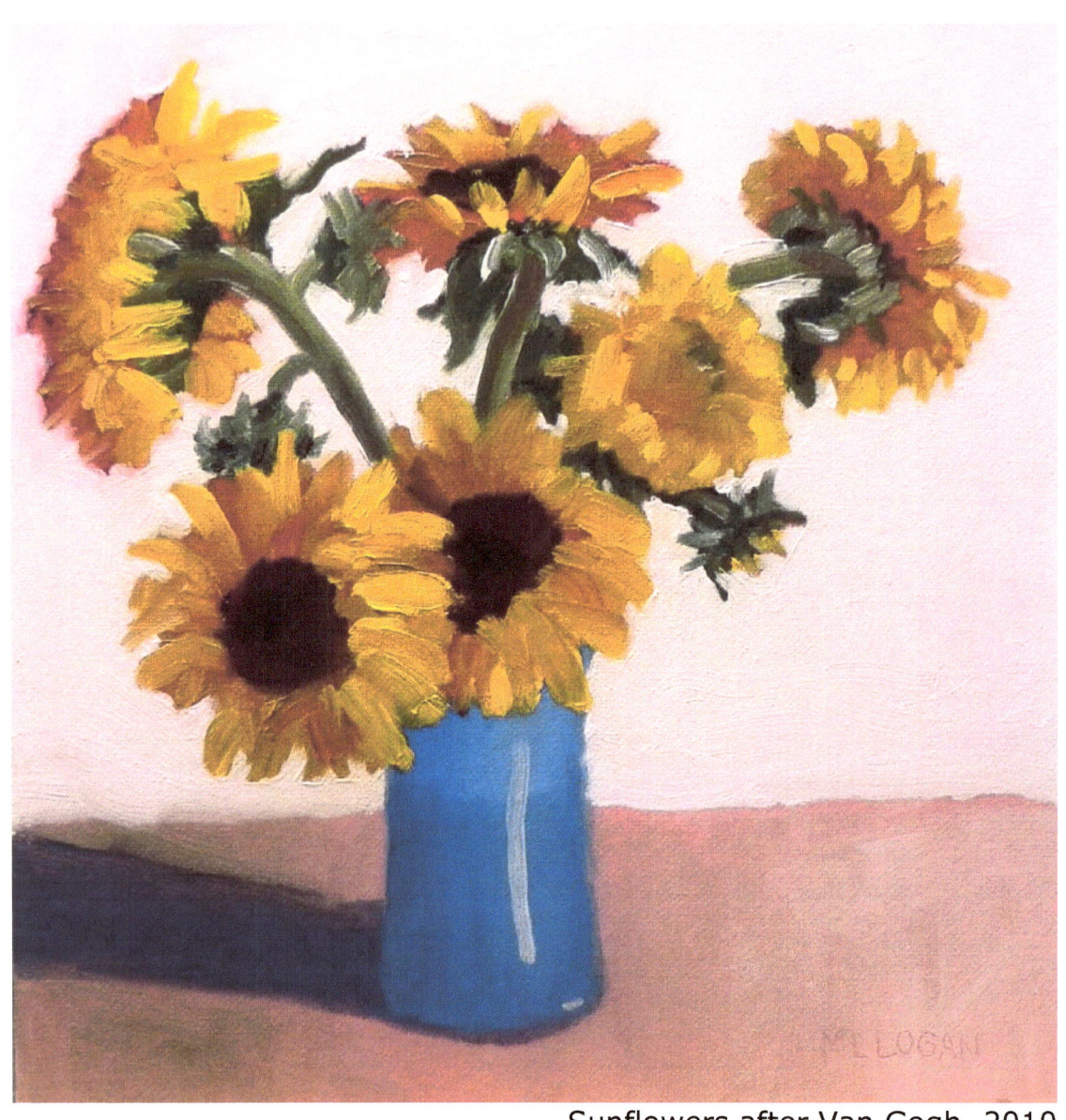

Sunflowers after Van Gogh, 2010

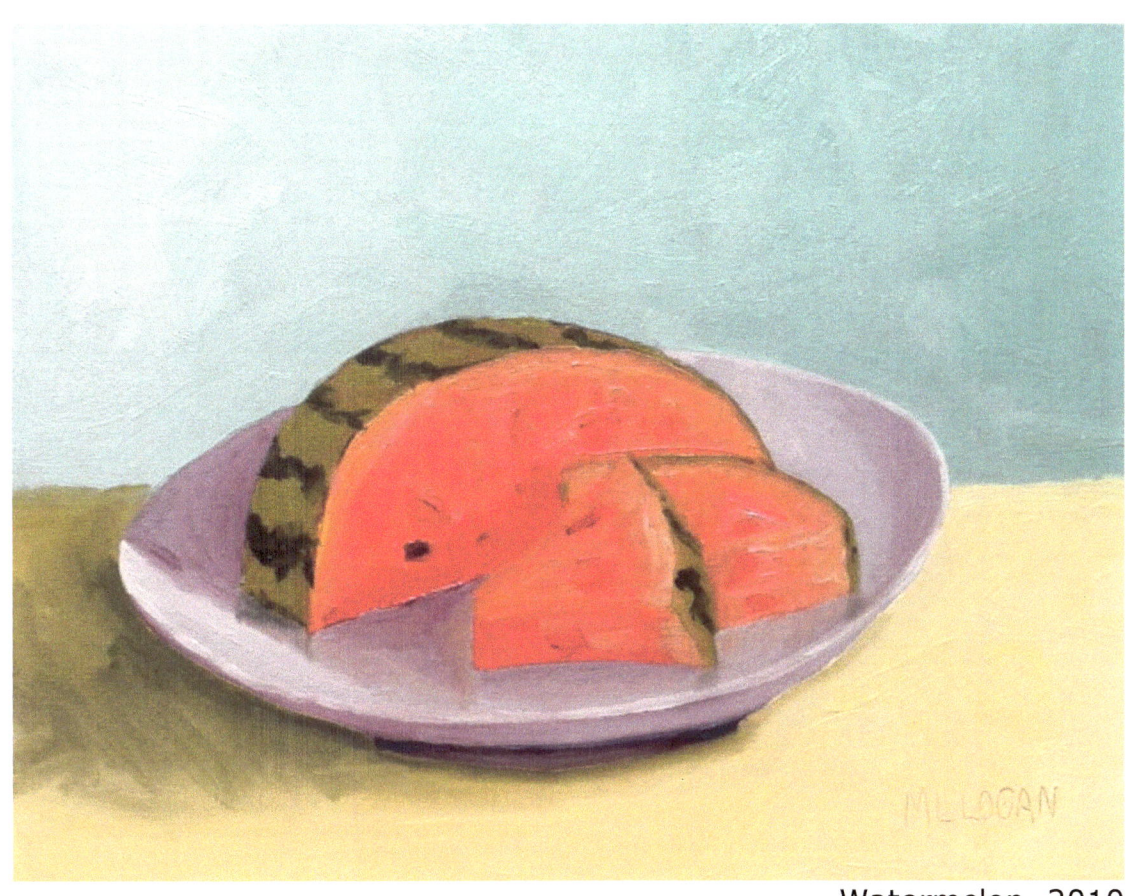

Watermelon, 2010

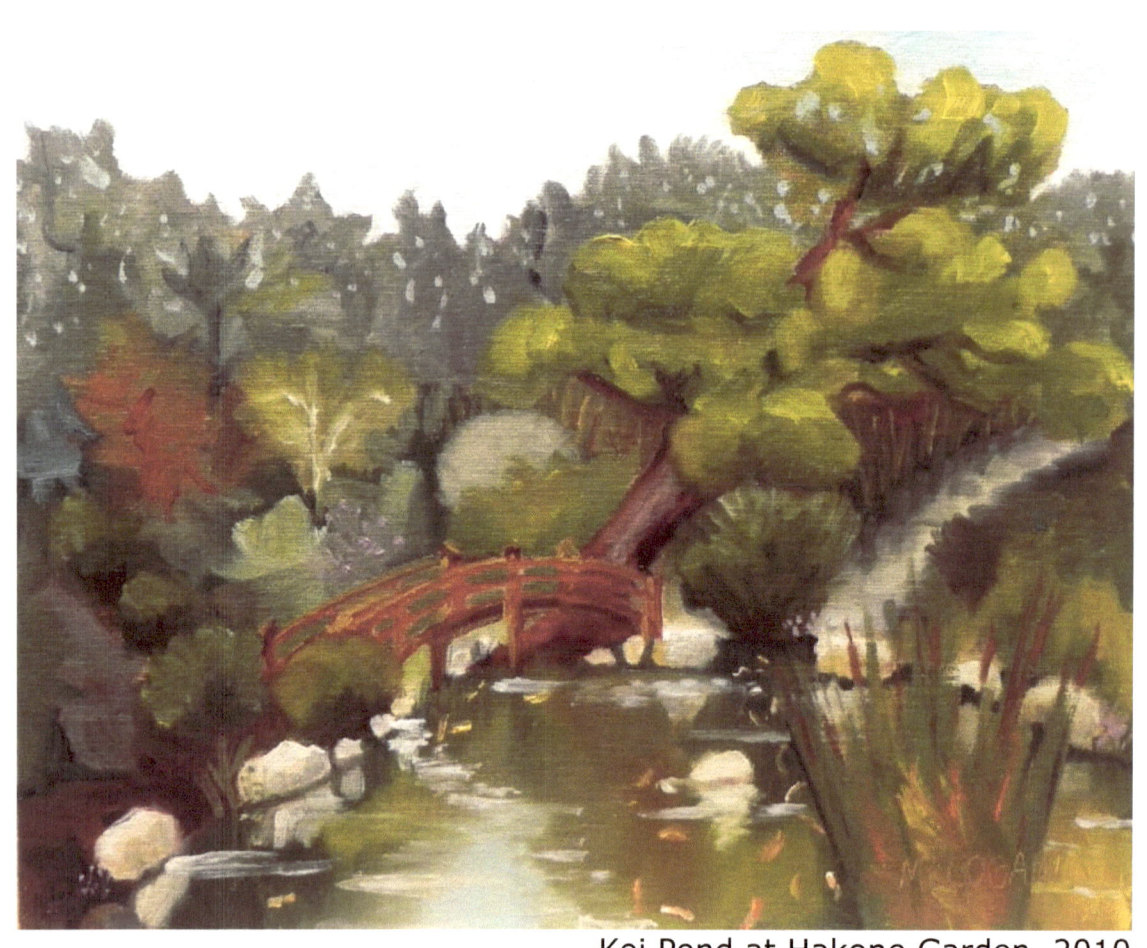

Koi Pond at Hakone Garden, 2010

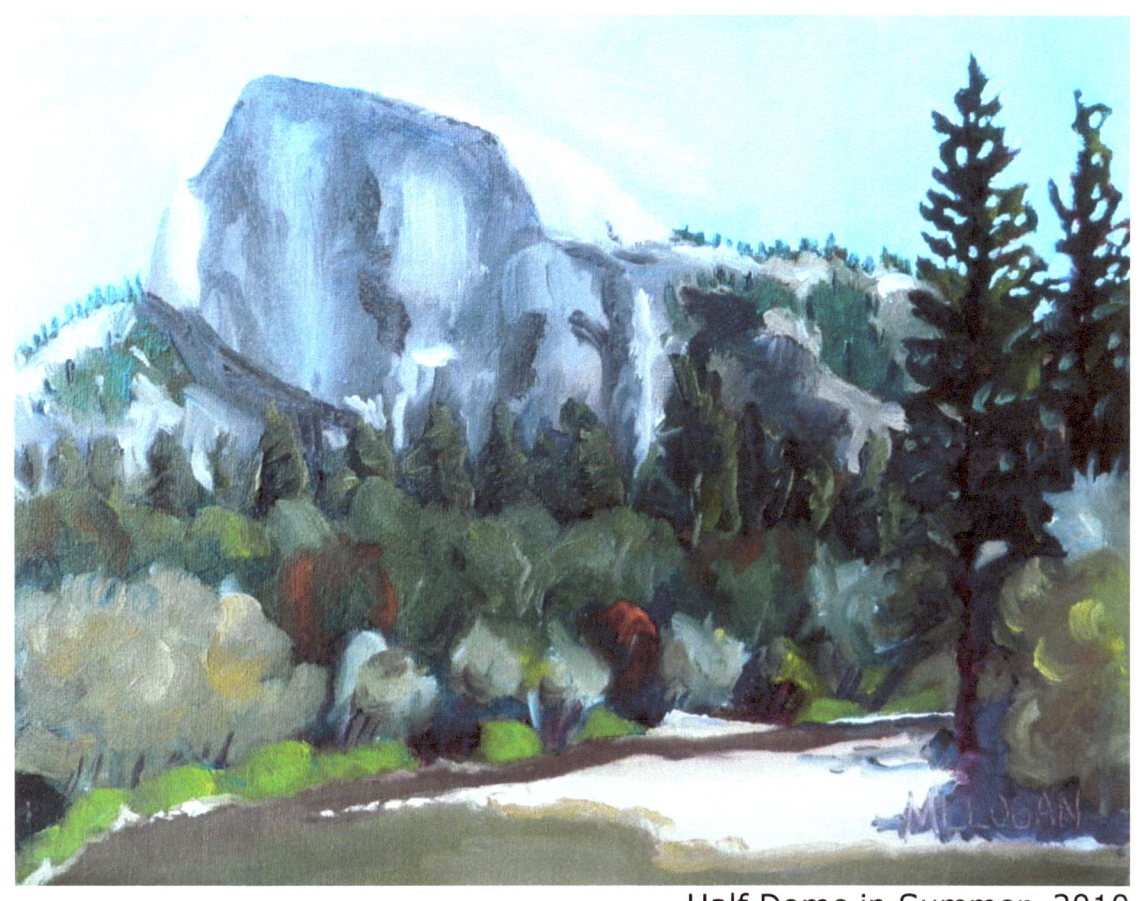

Half Dome in Summer, 2010

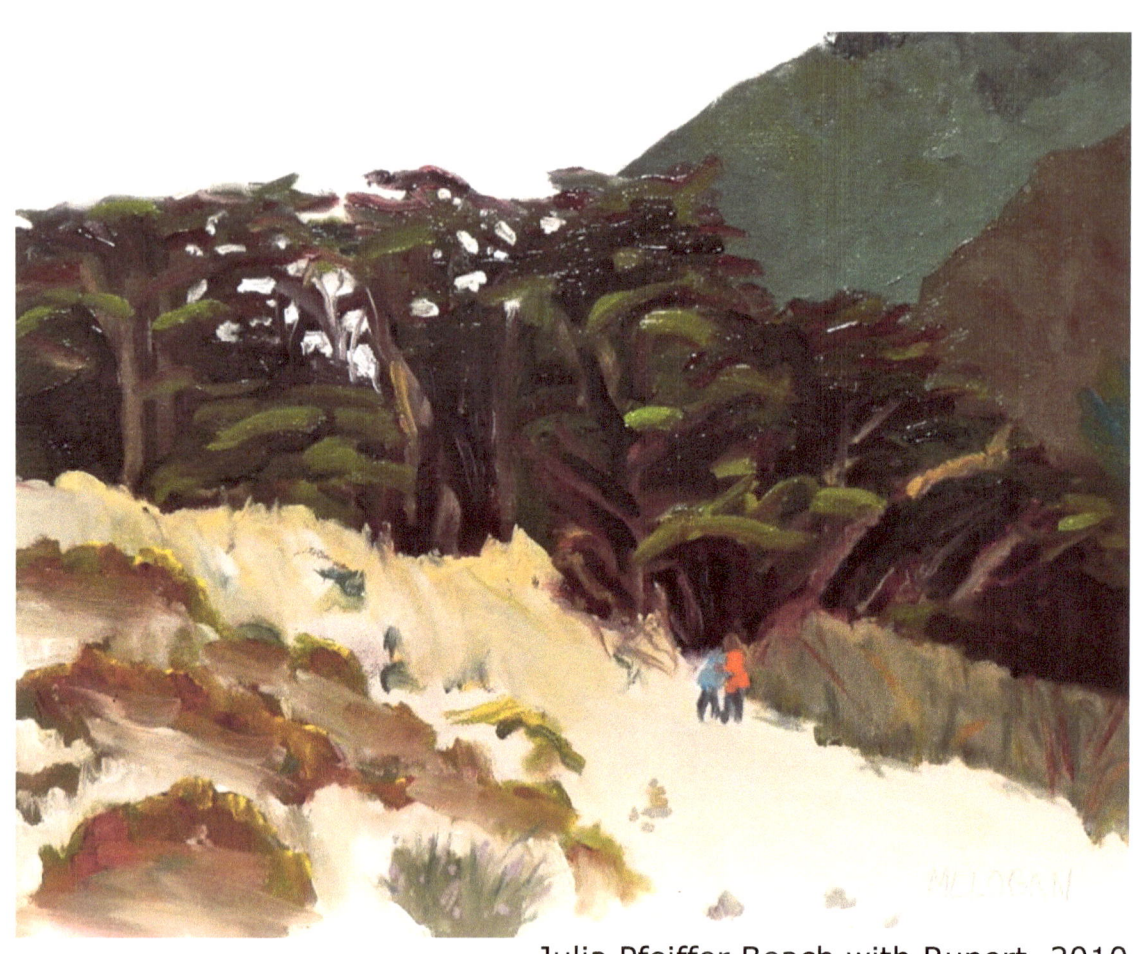

Julia Pfeiffer Beach with Rupert, 2010

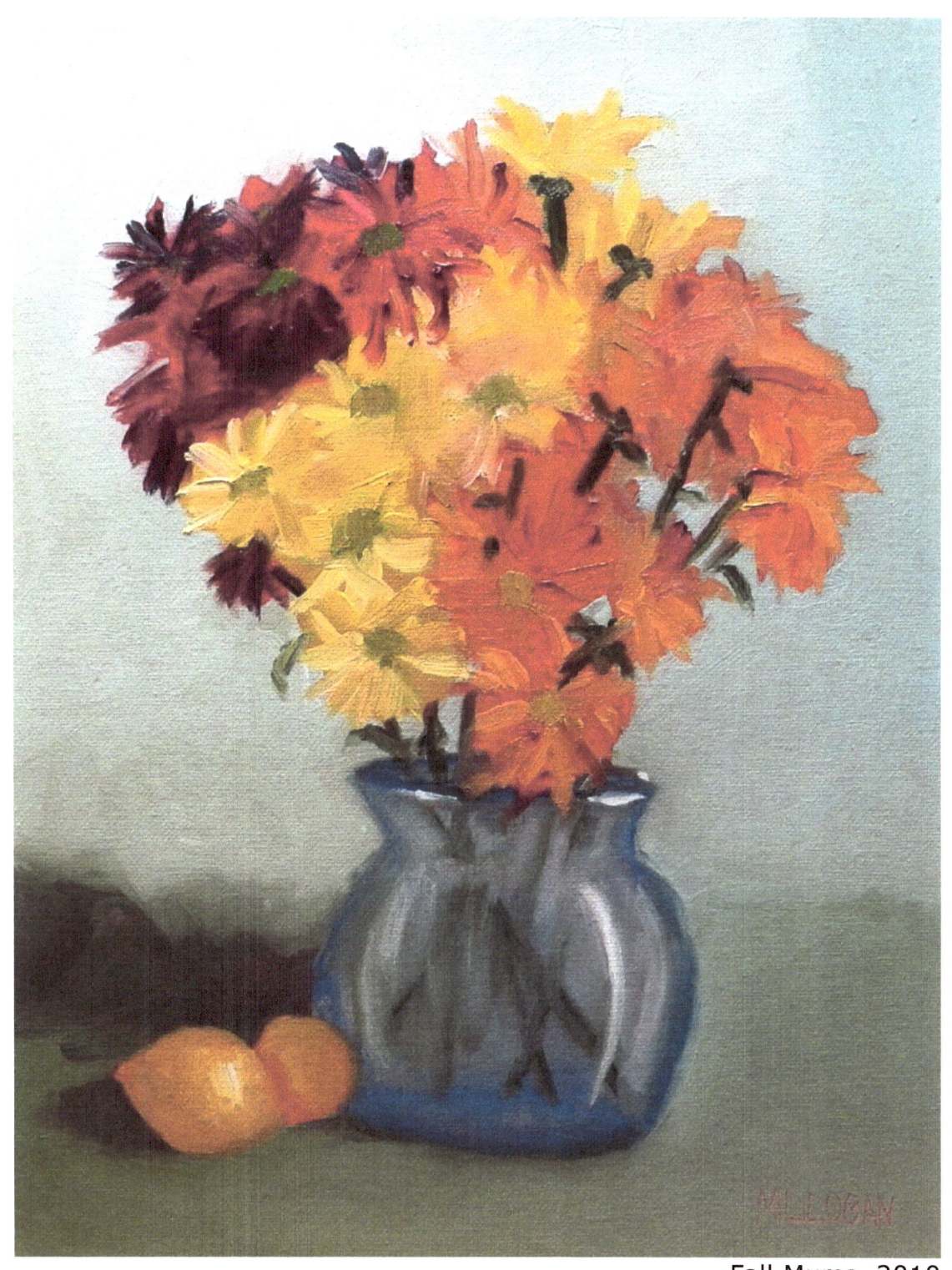

Fall Mums, 2010

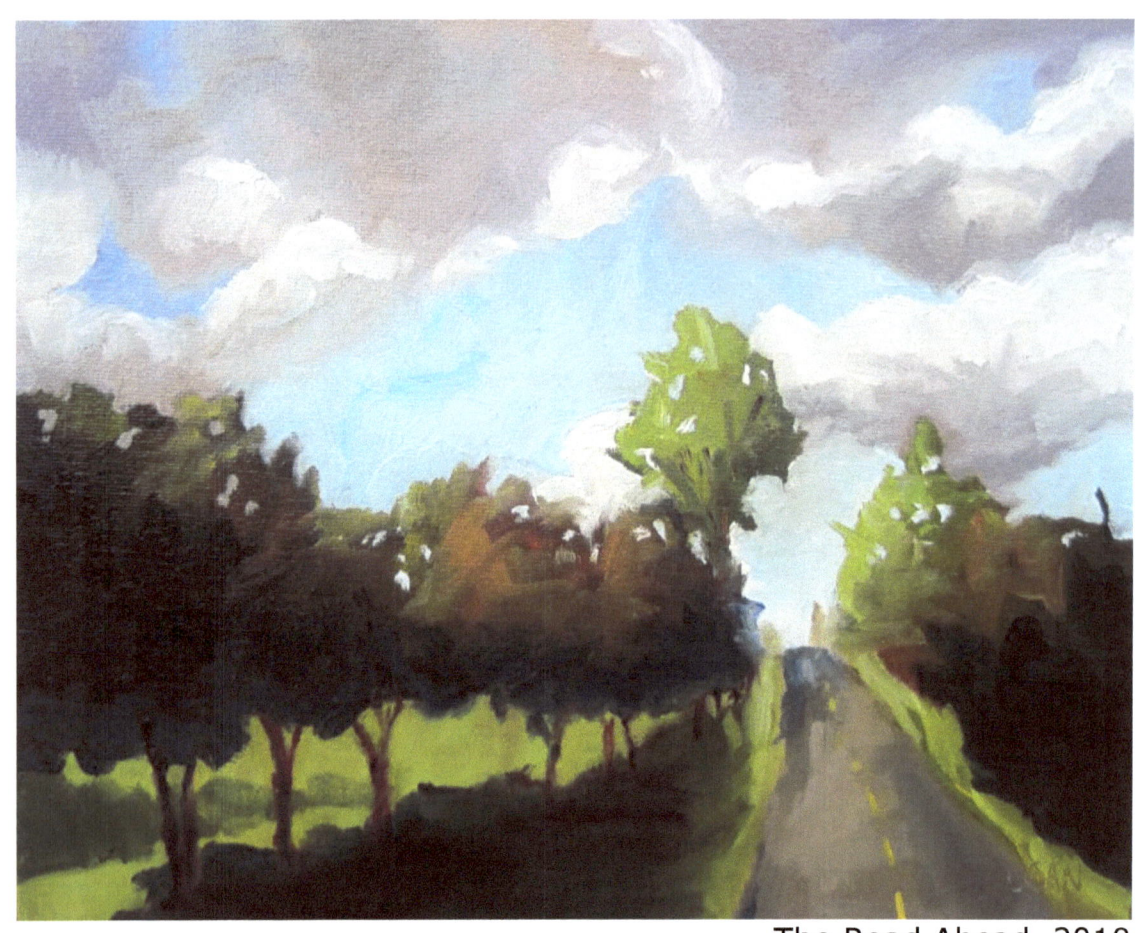

The Road Ahead, 2010

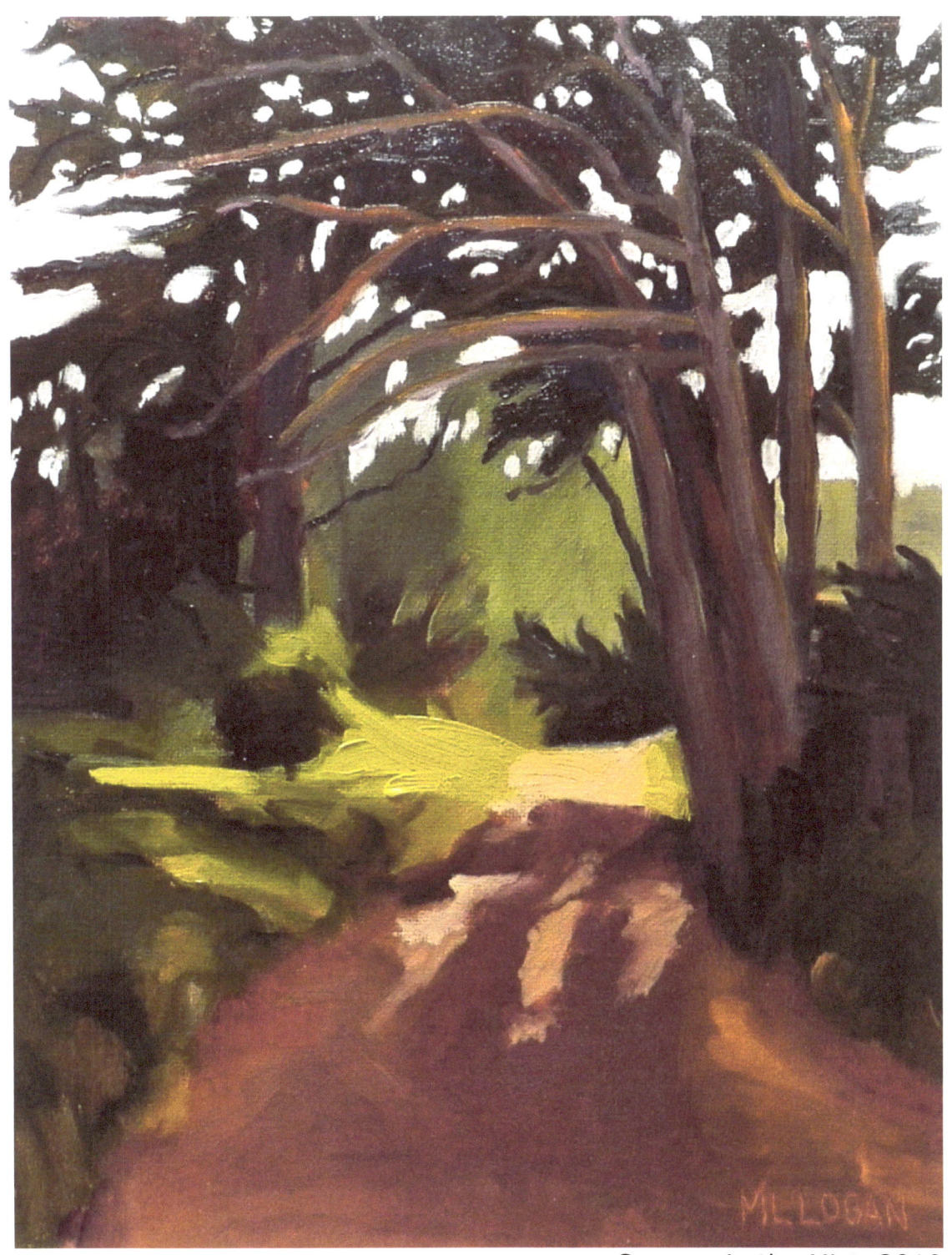

Cypress in the Mist, 2010

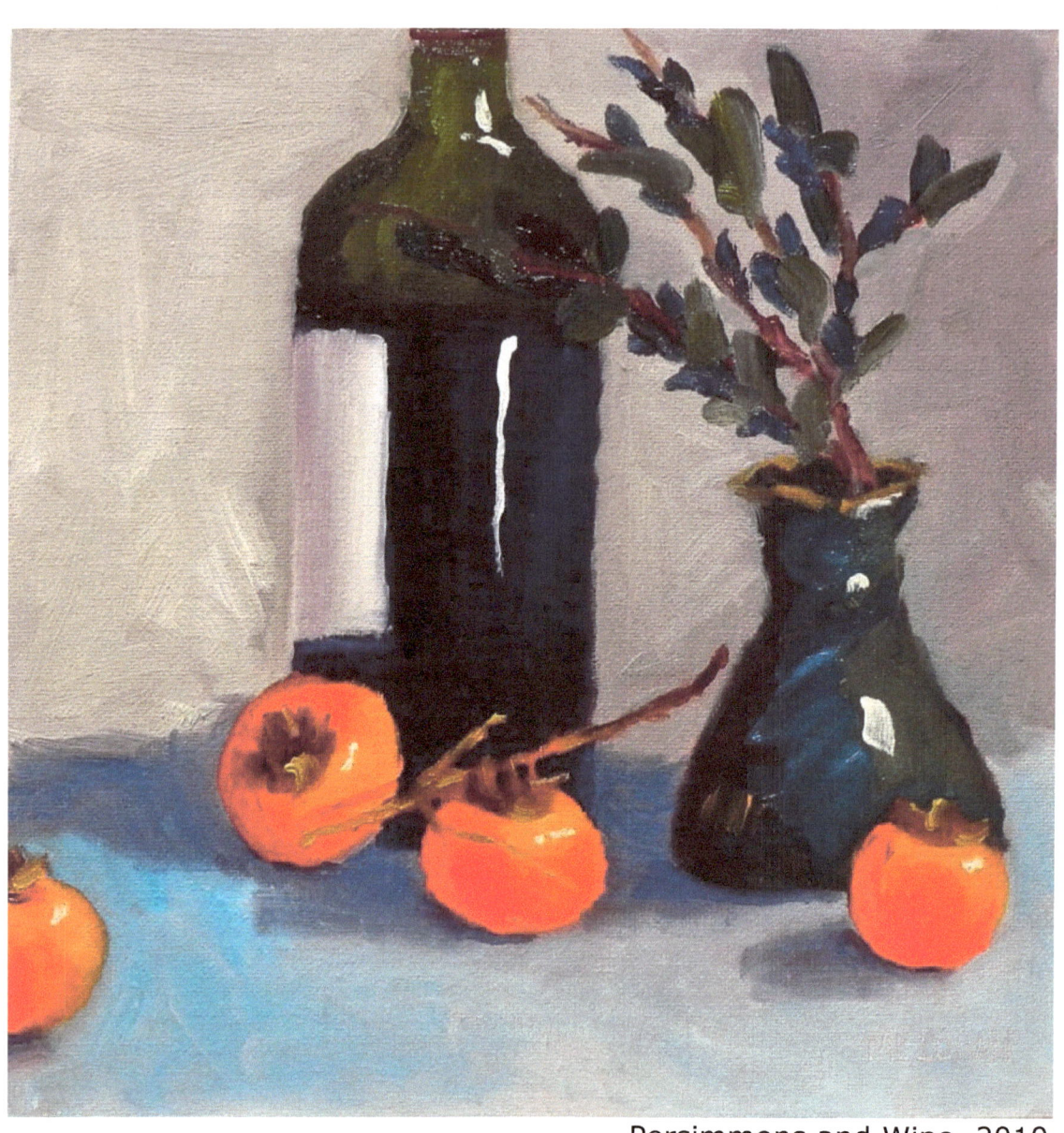

Persimmons and Wine. 2010

Catalogue Raisonnée

No.	Date	Title
1	2007	Ocean Beach Kite
2	2007	Land's End
3	2007	Cement Ship at Sunset
4	11/1/09	Stillwater Cove
5	11/7/09	Autumn Fields
6	11/12/09	The Upper Harbor, Santa Cruz
7	11/15/09	First Still Life
8	11/21/09	Paintbrushes Quick Study
9	11/21/09	Duck House Quick Study
10	1/13/10	Green Apple Study
11	1/23/10	Capitola Beach
12	1/28/10	Kerr to McHenry
13	1/30/10	After the Dutch Masters
14	2/4/10	Flowers with Green Apple
15	2/6/10	Field with Barn
16	2/13/10	Brown Jug with Berries
17	2/20/10	Corcoran Lagoon Quick Study
18	2/20/10	Landscape Quick Study
19	2/27/10	Teapot with Red Bowl
20	3/6/10	Near Watsonville
21	3/13/10	Plenty of Veggies
22	3/20/10	San Francisco Cityscape
23	3/27/10	Daisies
24	4/24/10	Mountain Lake
25	5/1/10	Davenport Cypress
26	5/15/10	Cupcakes
27	5/22/10	The Coast
28	5/22/10	Flowers from the Imagination
29	6/4/10	Año Nuevo
30	6/5/10	Arana Gulch
31	6/12/10	Quail Hollow Ranch
32	6/19/10	Corcoran Lagoon

33	7/3/10	Pink and Yellow Flowers in Jar
34	7/5/10	Golden Gate Botanical Gardens
35	7/18/10	Wilder Ranch Horse Barn
36	7/24/10	Agricultural fields near Sunset Beach
37	7/31/10	Sunflowers 1
38	8/4/10	Sunflowers after Van Gogh
39	8/25/10	Watermelon
40	8/27/10	Koi Pond at Hakone Garden
41	9/4/10	Half Dome in Summer
42	10/16/10	Julia Pfeiffer Beach with Rupert
43	10/24/10	Fall Mums
44	10/30/10	The Road Ahead
45	11/13/10	Cypress in the Mist
46	11/20/10	Persimmons and Wine